Permission!

Stop Competing and Start
Creating the Life You Want to Live

PRAISE FOR PERMISSION

"WOW...this book is brilliant! Nicole, walks next to us as a personal concierge who woos us with her riveting storytelling and painful truth. She invites us to peek behind the curtains of our lives and face the ugly truth of our setbacks. She then gives us the opportunity to lean in and create our future. I am so glad you she took off the mask and granted us permission to live as if this was our last day on earth. Thank you for the impact that you will have on millions of lives."

SIMON T. BAILEY, CEO of Brilliance Institute, Inc.
and author of *Release Your Brilliance*

"If you are in search of permission, Nicole will grant it. She takes you on her own personal and professional journey of self-acceptance and offers you tools to do the same."

DR. JACKIE FREIBERG, International bestselling author,
NUTS!, GUTS!, BOOM! And Nanovation

"In this inspiring and rich treasure trove of self-discovery, Nicole Matthews helps you discover the secrets you need to rise to new heights, to grow personally and to design a future that is truly limitless. Now you may use this book to become an award-winning architect of your entire life, one that is bold, brilliant and boundless."

PROFESSOR JOE GOLDBLATT, FRSA,
Queen Margaret University

"*Permission—Stop Competing & Start Creating the Life You Want to Live* is a home run! Nicole Matthews' story telling combines humor, heartbreak and business best practices into a must read for any woman who has ever felt stuck. You will find yourself rooting for her, identifying with her, and hopefully feeling motivated to take her recipe for success and apply it to your own life. Do yourself a favor and read Permission so you can design the life you want to live, yesterday!"

MARLEY MAJCHER, Boss at The Party Goddess!, Inc.
and author of *But Are You Making Any Money?*

Permission!

Stop Competing and Start
Creating the Life You Want to Live

NICOLE R. MATTHEWS

ARCHWAY
PUBLISHING

Archway Publishing books may be ordered through booksellers or by contacting:

Archway Publishing
1663 Liberty Drive
Bloomington, IN 47403
www.archwaypublishing.com
1-(888)-242-5904

ISBN: 978-1-4808-1194-2 (sc)
ISBN: 978-1-4808-1193-5 (hc)
ISBN: 978-1-4808-1195-9 (e)

Library of Congress Control Number: 2014918862

Printed in the United States of America.

Archway Publishing rev. date: 10/30/2014

Nana—You always told me I would; so I finally proved you right.

Ian and Elyse—If you are the only two children I will ever have the opportunity to help raise, my life will be doubly blessed.

Mom, Dad, Jodi and Steve—You are my everything.
I love you to the moon and back!

Some names have been changed in this book to protect the privacy of the good, the bad, and the "Oh, no, you didn't!"

Contents

Foreword . . . . *xi*

Here I Am . . . . *xiii*

Chapter 1   Are You the Architect of Your Own Life? 1

Chapter 2   What Is Keeping You Locked Up? 17

Chapter 3   Being Done and Letting Go 27

Chapter 4   Who Is in Your Circle? 43

Chapter 5   Permission 60

Chapter 6   What Is Your Authentic Intention? 73

Chapter 7   Impossible Versus I'm Possible 83

Chapter 8   All You Need Is Love 91

Chapter 9   The Big Ask 114

Chapter 10 Create Your Own Opportunities 128

Chapter 11 Permission Granted 146

Epilogue 171

Resources 179

Author Biography 181

Acknowledgements 185

Foreword

I'LL ADMIT IT—I WAS ONE OF THOSE WOMEN WHO walked up to Nicole after one of her endearing presentations with tears streaming down my face because I recognized I, too, was finally on the path that she had described, finally being the architect of my own life. It clearly had come with some costs, but there is nothing like realizing the potential of living a life congruent with your most sincere values and beliefs.

As Nicole discusses in her engaging presentations and authentic writing, being the architect of your own life requires a presence, engagement, and energy focused on a cause that incorporates not only serving others but also valuing and working at your own health and happiness. Unfortunately, we can get so caught up in being busy, putting out fires throughout the day, we find ourselves merely surviving instead of thriving.

In order to create and live the life and career of your dreams, we must design a blueprint for how we want to wake up each day and go after what's most important to us. A critical component of this plan must include the support of others, something that Nicole was blessed to learn early on in life. Whether you were born into a supportive family or you build your own through friends and community, support is essential to the soul and critical for our survival.

Although we are all surrounded by people, many of us in today's fast-paced society feel disconnected and at times isolated, an immediate trigger to the brain's stress response system. As Nicole describes through her own trials and triumphs, if we invest time and energy in strengthening the important relationships in our lives, we can lift each other as we climb, accomplishing even greater successes without compromising our health and happiness. It's a win-win-win—for ourselves, those we care about, and our world as a whole.

If you're ready to design the life and career of your dreams, I encourage you to learn from the path Nicole has created for herself, with the help of her friends and family. We can all benefit from leaning on each other a little bit more!

By the way, Nic, I never did get asked to my prom. Only now do I realize I should have gone anyway. If only I'd had your event planning guidance back then!

HEIDI HANNA, PhD
New York Times Best-Selling Author, Keynote Speaker
The SHARP Solution: A Brain-Based Approach for Optimal Performance

Here I Am

Give the girl the rights shoes,
and she can conquer the world.
—Marilyn Monroe

THE LENS I SEE LIFE THROUGH SEEMS TO BE COLORED
with opportunity. I learned at a fairly young age that in order to get
what I want in life, I have to create it myself. Now let's be clear. That's
not because I was abandoned as a child and forced to make my own
way—quite the opposite, in fact. I couldn't have grown up in a happier
home with more supportive parents. We're like a tribe. My parents are
the most accepting, encouraging, and unbelievably inclusive people
ever to have walked the planet. Our home knows no stranger—what
are you doing for Thanksgiving? Do you want to join us? I'm not
kidding! My sister and I sometimes meet people for the first time at
our Thanksgiving dinners because either my mom or dad met them
in their travels, and they learned that said stranger didn't have a place
to go for Turkey Day. My mother's greatest fear is that people will be
alone on a holiday, or worse yet, that they will never know a sense of
family. So, whether you are born into the tribe or you are just stopping
by, as long as you are comfortable doing the chicken dance before
dessert and partaking in the brutal gift exchange after dinner, you are
more than welcome for any holiday.

In addition to learning how to flap my wings and shake my tail feathers to a German folk dance on Turkey Day, my parents instilled in my sister and me a work ethic that not only demands commitment but also encourages casting a wide net in order to meet people, see places, and enjoy things. You work hard so you can play hard, which, thankfully, we did a lot of as children. My passport is full of stamps, and my list of stories of unique adventures is robust. In the spirit of anything-is-possible, I was raised with ambition and encouragement to live life to the fullest and to live with no regret. When you are given the great fortune of having a strong safety net with you at all times, it provides the permission for you to pursue goals, as crazy as they might seem, because you know the harness of your parents will always be there to catch you. Always knowing the net will appear has allowed me to take leaps off the platforms.

Now hold on. I can already hear you saying to yourself that it must be nice for someone to grow up in such a perfect world. Life is easy when you have a supportive home, family dinners, and the chicken dance. Yes, it is in fact. However, as perfect as everything seems on the outside, the voices in my head have a much different idea. It doesn't matter whose life you are looking at. What I know for sure is that it is pretty much smoke and mirrors. I have been diagnosed with clinical depression, which stems from such an intense lack of self-esteem and anxiety that my condition can be crippling at times. The girl with the perfect childhood found herself at twenty-five years old in the emergency room. There I had an emotional breakdown after years of never feeling good enough, never living up to some idealized version of who I should be, and never feeling like there might be a chance for me. I knew it was bad when they moved me to that special area in the back of the emergency room where only the psychotic patients are treated, away from the broken fingers, heart attacks, and common colds. While a person visits Crazy Land, a variety of doctors and health-care professionals come in who pretend to understand what the patient is going through. They try to do a lot of reassuring that "you

are good enough, smart enough and doggone it, people like you!"
(Apparently, mental health treatment was taken from a *Saturday Night Live* skit.) I remember the doctor coming in and asking me if I felt sad. Yes, I felt very sad. Of course, they wanted to know if I planned on hurting myself, others, or pets. I was a member of PETA for several years, so I assured her the puppies were safe. I never thought about killing myself, but I did long to take a nap that would rival that of Sleeping Beauty. I just wanted to sleep the sadness away. The doctor asked me if I wanted to be admitted for observation, because she could tell that I had gotten to the point of no longer being able to cry. I just chose to stare at the wall. My eyes were dry and puffy. Still, I had the great ability to find the humor in every situation. This included wondering why the doctor would be wearing a giant white banana clip in her hair. Which one of us really had the problem here? The year 1985 called; it wanted its hair accessory back! Even in a dark depression, the details never got by me.

My depression was not the fault of my parents, my home setting, or my childhood. I believe that this has everything to do with me, and the fact that for way too long I stood in my own way, caved in, and learned how to play the game of comparing my ability, my looks, and my self-worth to everyone else's. How could a girl who essentially grew up in utopia be cursed? Easy—I gave way too much energy to worry, anxiety, and the voices in my head.

When I set out to write this book, it was not because I wanted to come across as having everything figured out and am now living a charmed life. In fact, it's the exact opposite. It's my struggles within the framework of a seemingly ideal childhood that compelled me to share my story. I often wonder if such anxiety and lack of self-esteem could happen to me, given the *Leave It To Beaver* childhood I had, what is life like for those who had a childhood with far more challenges and far less support?

As I've been speaking around the country, I have been finding that after every presentation, several women have been coming up to me in tears. I always appreciate engaging with the audience, but these experiences were different. Instead of just asking for my business card so we could stay connected, these women were telling me their stories. Over and over what they would end up saying is that they felt like I had given them permission, through my own story, to start living the life they want and to make changes in their lives. Permission? I was simply sharing a few chapters of my life. How could my own experience be the permission they were seeking? As I gave more presentations, I encountered more tears. I realized that instead of hitting the nail on the head for these women, I was helping them to remove the nail that had been hammered into the same board for so long. Rarely, when you remove a nail from a board, does the nail come out straight. Instead, it shows the friction and the bends that weather, age, and the hammer have caused. These women, with their tears, were ready to have their nails pulled from their board. If permission was what they needed, permission was granted.

I wish I could tell you that I have figured out completely how to have successful relationships with men, how to run a business, and how to forge my place in the world. If that is what you are looking for, then you are in the wrong place. Please be sure to forward me the title of the book where you find all the answers! Instead, what I want to share with you is the real, honest, blood, sweat, and tears it has taken to reach thirty-nine years of age and finally feel like I am on the path to a self-designed fulfilling life.

Let me get the ugly truth of out of the way, so that I feel like I can move forward with authenticity to write this book. At thirty-seven years old, I faced not only the deepest heartbreak I could ever imagine, but also financial instability that forced me to move back home with my parents. I boomeranged back to my childhood bedroom with very little money and a heart so broken that I didn't know if even superglue could put my Humpty Dumpty back together again. I learned in 2011 that the only thing I could really ever count on was myself, a small but mighty group of girlfriends, and my unbelievable family, who opened their doors and let me come home again. Over the past two years, I have cried; I have healed; I have put money in savings; and I have kept my motivation to be an entrepreneur. Standing on this side of the sunset of the past two years, I am profoundly proud that what I was able to survive has indeed not killed me, but instead made me stronger. Life is hard at times. I will not sugarcoat the fact that I have had plenty of challenges. However, faith in myself has been the prescription I needed to move from grieving to thriving.

Clearly, there have been numerous setbacks, roadblocks, and a lot of friction, but something deep in me has always dreamed of a life that is full of opportunity, unique experiences, and self-creation. This is the path I have chosen to pursue, and if my story can help you to forge your own path and seek your own opportunities in spite of whatever challenge or chapter you are now experiencing, then I am glad you have chosen to read this book.

Here's the quick secret to it all: A truly fulfilled life starts with giving yourself permission to stop competing in your personal life and in business and instead start creating your own opportunities. What do you really have to lose?

When the Going Gets Tough

Once I finally got the voices in my head to quiet down, I realized that when the going gets tough, the tough start creating their own opportunities. If you want to follow the yellow brick road, you need to carve your own path and paint it with gold. Being passive and letting life just happen to you seems like such a waste of space. Again, I feel like clarification is necessary.

By no means do I wake up every day doing backflips, searching for rainbows, and petting my unicorn. There are plenty of days when I have to find the courage and motivation to get up and face the world. There have been plenty of dark periods, but it is in those darkest moments that I strive to walk toward the light. As I look back on my life, I see that I've forged my biggest changes after some of my most heartrending times. When my heart is most broken, I'm able to make the most significant changes. This takes time, but I eventually get there. Knowing that the only way to move forward is to go through a situation and not around it, I've had to dig very deep inside and silence the doubt and sadness.

Until recently, I lived with such insane anxiety that I would make myself physically ill. My anxiety was always self-inflicted because I allowed doubt and lack of self-esteem to creep into my mind. Was I really worthy? Did he really like *me*, or was this just a big trick? My ability to go from zero to one hundred on the anxiety scale was exponentially higher when a man-person was involved. I can mark time by the places I've made myself throw up, and evenings with a man that have had to be cut short because my anxiety got the better of me. After being unsuccessful in several anxiety-producing relationships, I believe I will know when I've found the "one" because I won't want to throw up in the parking lot! What has curbed my anxiety has been the decision to take an anti-anxiety medicine. It's not something I'm proud of or a nugget I share with most people (until the writing of this book!), but I have to admit that not living my days with crippling anxiety and self-doubt has helped me in ways I could never imagine. If you need permission to see your doctor to discuss a "happy pill" to help you cope, permission is granted. Not being tired, depressed, and spinning out of control is a change I finally welcomed and a decision I am delighted I made a few years ago. Do I want to be on an anti-anxiety medication forever? Certainly not! But I do welcome that in this chapter of my life, I have been given a tool to help provide balance. When you are fighting so hard against yourself daily, it's hard to make progress. I've chosen to move forward and swim with the tide rather than against it.

I'm not particularly unusual, but what I have found that makes me different is my commitment to creating my own opportunities. I figure out what I want, and I make a plan to get it. After living near London a few years ago, I discovered that there are two kinds of people from England. There are those who sit in the same pub, on the same stool, with the same friends, drinking the same pints on the same schedule, almost every day of the year. These are what I call the "I wish I coulds." Contrary to those types are the English people who are committed to seeing the world. They're nomads. They either make sure to travel frequently, or they pick up and move to a foreign country and make a life for themselves away from the rain and monotony of England. For the record, by picking up this book you have engaged with the biggest Anglophile on the planet. If I could snap my fingers and live anywhere, it would be in England again. I'm convinced that the land Her Majesty rules will always be one of the greatest loves of my life. So it is only through my personal experience and utter respect and admiration for England that I can comment on the two groups of people you will find. I decided long ago that I didn't want to be sitting in the pub with the "I wish I coulds."

What group are you in? Are you stuck on the barstool, wishing for a different life, or are you boarding the opportunity plane?

Focus on Creating Great Opportunities and Collecting Stories

What I hope you will garner by reading this book is that only you can design the life you want to live. Success really has very little do to with your education, your current income, or your relationship status. If you really want something bad enough, you will figure out a way to make it happen. The greatest differentiator among people is drive.

I'm not an early bird; I don't get up before sunrise to start building the empire. I don't work out like I'm a contestant on *The Biggest Loser*, nor do I have as many figures in my bank account as I would want. But am I working toward all these things? Yes! Instead of exhausting myself with obsessing about my waist size, my credit score, and my company's P&L, I instead focus on creating unique experiences in my life that will lead to great stories and priceless memories. It's amazing how circumstances somehow line up when you design your life based more on experience and less on financial gain. I create my own opportunities like "accessories" now. These accessories go with every outfit and are the finishing touches on every design. I love helping people to discover how they, too, can create their own opportunities. I've carved a niche in the special events and concierge industry by producing my own events. Additionally, I now coach other planners and business owners on how to produce their own revenue-generating events. I also spend a lot of time helping my university students to design the life they want instead of the life they think they are supposed to live.

I was recently helping a colleague in the Career Development office at a local university with mock interviews. She asked me to conduct interviews with current students to evaluate their readiness to interview for life in the real world. I met this delightful young lady whom we will call Beatrice, who is just weeks away from graduating. Poor Beatrice doesn't really know who she wants to be when she grows up, but she was playing the part of the aspiring job seeker very well. I could tell that outside influences such as her family, her church, and her obligations were encouraging her to graduate and get a "real job." Through our conversation, it was obvious that what Beatrice really needed was permission to do exactly the opposite of what everyone was telling her to do.

Instead of encouraging her to jump on the corporate escalator, I asked her if she ever considered throwing everything she needed in a backpack and traveling the world. Her response, "Yes, I would love to, but …" Before she could shower me with the reasons why not, I stopped her and said, "I give you permission to do just that." The relief that flooded over her was tangible. This darling girl was being molded by everyone around her to choose *their* path. I encouraged her to choose her own. How will she ever figure out who she wants to be if she doesn't allow herself to get lost in the big world? There's no rush. Why should she have to graduate on May 31 and start working at a mediocre job on June 1? What's wrong with taking some time for self-exploration and putting all that theory college professors teach you into real-world application?

I encouraged Beatrice to put stamps in her passport before she puts her name on a business card. Because Beatrice is interested in event planning, I may hire her someday. In my role as a potential future employer, I told Beatrice that I would not hire her until she could prove that she had spent time traveling and enjoying unique experiences. I can only hope she listens to her authentic intention instead of the voices around her.

I hope that as you read this book, you will start to listen to that inner voice in your head that is telling you exactly how you would like to design your life. This has nothing to do with how much money you have. I've learned that the more you have, the more problems come along. Even if I handed you a billion dollars right this minute, could you tell me what you want to do with your life? We all know that just sitting on the couch and cashing your checks would get boring after a while. Instead, I want to give you the permission to start not only dreaming, but also putting a plan into place to move one step closer to really living your life the way you truly want.

CHAPTER ONE
Are You the Architect of Your Own Life?

"You are far too smart to be
the only thing standing in your way.
—Jennifer Freeman

AFTER BEING HIRED AS A CONSULTANT IN LONDON
for a four-month project back in 2000, I returned to San Diego, where
I began the big job search. I had been a Bohemian for months, so I was
pressured to get a "real job." I applied for a position in a high-profile
law firm. To my delight, I was hired as the marketing manager. The
firm had an impressive reputation, and my new position was the ideal
job in the corporate sandbox. The problem was that on the third day
I remember having a conversation with myself that started off with,
"I think I've made a huge mistake ..." On day three, I knew I was in
the wrong spot. I stayed five years! Was I a glutton for punishment?
No, but I just didn't think there was anything beyond this great job
in corporate America.

I was lucky, because I was an administrator and did not have to
reside on Cubicle Island. Within weeks of joining the firm, I recall
being in an administrators' meeting, where we had to discuss how
much perfume people (translation: hourly staff) could wear, and how

many personal photos were allowed on their desks. I was intrigued; was someone going to be hired as the perfume police and sniff the staff as they entered the building every day? How much was too much cologne, and whose nose was going to serve as the Richter scale for scents? It was decided that each cubicle could be decorated with two personal photos; so much for free expression. Months later, I found myself in a planning meeting for an upcoming firm retreat. At the meeting, I was told by a senior attorney that we didn't want to bring in a keynote speaker on work and life balance because that wasn't something they were really encouraging for the young associates. Like residencies in medical schools, law firms require young associates to work extremely long hours. After all, if the partners had to endure lives without balance, why should the current generation break the mold?

Year one of my tenure at the law firm was a blur. In year two, I became bitter and accumulated emotional baggage because I realized that this firm was probably the epitome of corporate America. Who wouldn't want to work on the twenty-eighth floor, have a bay view, a hefty salary, and afford BMW cars like they were BMX bikes? My business card always warranted respect when I handed it out, because the firm had such a prestigious reputation. Although I appreciated the opportunity I was given to work for such a desirable company, I couldn't help but keep asking myself, "Is this all there is?"

One of the most profound moments I had while working at the firm came during a salary negotiation. Within a year of joining the firm, the director of marketing left for another opportunity. For over a year, I assumed the responsibility of that position, while also maintaining my position as marketing manager. The marketing coordinator left a few months later, so for almost eight months, I essentially ran the marketing department with the help of an executive assistant. When it came time for my annual review, I prepared myself to meet with the senior leadership. After having reported directly to them during the absence of a director, I felt comfortable and confident heading into my evaluation. I made sure that I had a strong list of my accomplishments, which included producing more events than the firm had ever executed, all while being significantly under budget. I was also carrying the responsibility of three positions. I felt that given my competent abilities and contributions, it was a viable time to negotiate for an increase in salary and promotion of title. I spent time researching similar positions in the legal marketing industry, so I was able to propose a fair compensation structure and promotion of title and responsibility. I had prepared and done my homework. They listened to me as I presented my self-evaluation and accomplishments. When I finished, all that they said was, "We will take your proposal into consideration." I was a little taken back by their lack of enthusiasm for my presentation, but felt confident in my abilities and efforts.

Shortly after making my way back to my office, the senior partner knocked on my door. He came into my office and asked me point blank, "What are you trying to do?" I had to repeat the question to myself to ensure that I really heard what he said. What was I trying to do? "I'm negotiating my salary and asking for a promotion to honor the contributions I have made to the firm in the last year," I told him. Basically, like it or lump it, the message was that senior management would tell me what my salary increase would be because I wasn't supposed to negotiate. He went on to tell me that although I had been working hard, it was unrealistic to think that I should be compensated for balancing three positions and delivering an event portfolio under budget.

I grew up in a time when women were beginning to assume and perceive themselves to be equal to men. The generations before fought hard so I could sit equally at the boardroom table. I'm grateful for the sacrifices that my grandmother and mother's generations made so that I could have career options beyond teacher, nurse, or secretary. Their sacrifices are not lost on me. Still, I would be remiss if I didn't admit that I have never felt inferior or unqualified in the workplace. I sat in meetings with top clients and the managing partner of the firm, and it never dawned on me that I didn't belong there because I was a woman. In my mind, once I was hired, I was invited to the table. Competency means more to me than whether your genitals determine if you wear trunks or a bikini at the pool.

Admittedly, I was stunned that I was actually being challenged on my decision to negotiate and advocate for my contributions. Would this same conversation have taken place had my name been Nicholas?

Economist Linda Babcock of Carnegie Mellon University states that through her research she has discovered, "It turns out that when [a woman does] negotiate, it can backfire. She may be successful in getting the money, but people do not like her. They think she is too demanding. And this can have real consequences for a woman's career." When I asked the senior partner if he negotiated for his compensation, all I got was "Yes, but ..."

Six months after I attempted to negotiate, the firm hired a new director of marketing, and I continued to clock my time in a fancy office on the twenty-eighth floor. More than ever, though, my discontent with corporate America continued to fester. That year I was given a small bump to my salary, but it was a token compared to what I had contributed. To say that I felt a tad diminished is an understatement.

I'm a big believer that the universe always puts you where you are supposed to be because there is a lesson to be learned. Even though it was a painful lesson, what the universe was reminding me was that I was *not* being the architect of my own life. When I didn't receive the raise and promotion that I was seeking, I retreated. Shame on me! You can't design the life you want to live by becoming a wallflower. I was agreeing to play small if I chose to stay at the law firm longer than it served me. It was on that day that I decided the only way up was to get out. I had a great job, so I knew it wouldn't improve the situation to just seek other employment. Instead, what I finally allowed to be heard was the voice in my head seeking self-employment. Jumping ship and earning a high-profile position with another firm or in a different industry was not going to benefit me well in the long run.

The easy road would have been to apply elsewhere, but that's just moving a set of problems to a different address. A new company might not be talking about perfume sprays or personal photo counts, but it would bring more bureaucracy, which I remembered makes me break out in hives.

I realized that I might not be able to hang my shingle as a business owner the very next day, but this salary negotiation experience became the fuel to put the plan in motion. Every great journey begins with a single step. On that day, I laced up my shoes and stood on the starting line. Never again was I going to be at the mercy of someone else deciding my value.

Being the architect of your own life is not always easy, but when you finally have that moment of clarity—when you realize that what you are doing is no longer working—this situation becomes your permission to make a change. The first step in recovery is always admitting there is a problem. Corporate America and I were having a big problem with each other, so I knew it was time to change.

My outlook on the firm changed significantly thanks to the support of my new marketing director. When Ramona joined the team, she was picking up fractured pieces. She inherited a team that was not particularly close and couldn't be more opposite in their work and communication styles. Sensing the need to bridge the gaps, Ramona hired a communication style expert by the name of Mindy Bortness of Communication Works, Inc. to conduct a *DISC* assessment on the team. DISC is a personal assessment tool that is used to improve work efficiency, communication, and teamwork. We all took our online DISC tests and then had to meet for a one-day department retreat where this chick Mindy was going to tell us all about ourselves. Yawn!

I arrived first to the retreat and found a binder with my name on it located in the seat I was assigned. I immediately flipped it open and started scanning the material. "Nicole tends to be intolerant of people who seem ambiguous or think too slowly." And "Nicole will work long hours until a tough problem is solved. After it is solved, Nicole may become bored with any routine work that follows." Mindy noticed that I had opened the binder, and she politely asked me to wait until the others had joined us before reading ahead. I was already irritated that I had to be part of this exercise, and now I was being paced. Not a great start! As the morning progressed, Mindy explained all about the DISC assessment, how each of us has our own communication style, and how that impacts those we work with and our own level of efficiency. No shock to me, my assessment showed I was a *High D*, which stands for dominant. According to the report, I am decisive, venturesome, inquisitive, and responsible when it comes to decision-making. When talking about High D's, the motto is, "Be brief, be focused, and then be gone." We aren't your touchy-feely, sit around, and hug it out kind of people. We get bored easily, and are sociable only by our own decision. We like you or we don't. There isn't really much gray in our sight. We aren't the cranky-pants in the room, but we like to take the lead, not for our ego, but because we want to move the process along.

The hair raised on my arms as I read through my binder. I was finally reading the Nicole bible, and those pages explained why I am the way I am. Mindy told me exactly what I had been feeling, "You are a square peg in a round hole." Cue the choir singers and the fireworks. We finally had an explanation of why I felt like working at the law firm was such a rub. I realized on that day that there is absolutely nothing wrong with the law firm (except, perhaps, their dislike of perfume), and that this girl was indeed the problem. It's so easy to point the finger and say there must be something wrong with everyone else. However, on that day, around a table of DISC assessment binders, I was given permission to no longer try to fit in. Talk about being empowered! Ramona's intention for conducting the DISC assessment was not to force me out; instead, she was just trying to figure out how to manage this motley crew. Little did I know that this High D's binder was going to lay the groundwork and give me permission to move on.

Ramona allowed each of us on the team to work with Mindy

individually for one-on-one coaching. I already had an inclination that my heart was leaning toward entrepreneurship. Fortunately, Ramona was gracious enough to allow me to talk about anything I wanted with Mindy. (Wink, wink!) The first time I met with her, away from the office, she validated everything that I was feeling. I didn't fit at the law firm, and that was perfectly acceptable. I would do more damage to myself if I stayed than I ever would by risking self-employment. For the next few weeks, Mindy and I crafted a plan that involved my exit strategy. Finally, I felt like I had a purpose again.

When you finally give yourself permission to make a change, it can be both scary and invigorating. Although I was committed to starting my own business, the reality was that this did not happen overnight. In fact, it took more than two years before it actually happened. I can't thank Ramona enough, because by sharing with her my ultimate goal of starting my own business, she was incredibly supportive. I was very good at my job, so she didn't have to worry about my commitment to the firm. This allowed me a lot of autonomy and flexibility to start building my business on the side. Ramona wasn't intimidated by the thought of my leaving and knowing she would ultimately have to replace me. Instead, what she saw was a spark in my eyes that she had never seen before, and she did everything she could as not only my manager but also as my friend to help me get where I was supposed to be. Ramona and Mindy are both a very important part of my story, and we are still friends to this day. They remain a couple of my biggest cheerleaders.

Being the architect of your own life forces you to start living life, not just letting life live you. You have to be present, engaged, and always committed to a bigger cause—your personal happiness! I had to draft a blueprint, like every good architect, that illustrated what it was that I wanted to build. It was time to manifest a life outside of corporate America.

As I said, from the light-bulb moment with Mindy when I realized I was meant to be not an employee but an entrepreneur, it was another two years before I actually left the firm. This was certainly not as fast as I was hoping, but the timing wasn't right for me to just up and leave at the time. I needed to get my ducks in a row. I also needed enough regular business before hanging out my own shingle full-time. I might not be in favor of rules, but I am in favor of being able to pay my bills, so the timeline moved slower than I had hoped. I was just glad I finally had a plan and could see the light at the end of the tunnel. When you know the timing is right, you will finally step off the platform.

Do you know someone who always complains about the boss? For some reason people like that are the ones who always work for the most vindictive, cruelest, out-to-get-me bosses on the planet. I've been fortunate enough to have had a long career with many jobs, starting all the way back with selling muffins out of a basket to companies in tall downtown buildings, most recently with a firm called Posh Nosh. To this day, with a glance and a blink of the eye, I can spot a blueberry muffin versus an orange-cranberry one. Not once have I ever worked for someone who was "out to get me" or the "biggest idiot on the planet." Have I loved every person I worked with? Probably not, but I certainly have never worked for a jerk I felt was trying to undermine my success. Even working at the law firm, I knew it was my rub with the environment, not the people, that made the job a challenge for me.

It never makes sense to me how some people can continually point fingers at their bosses being the problem instead of themselves. There is a great saying: "Point one finger at someone else, and there are three fingers pointed back at you." Never is this more true than with the people who take no personal responsibility for their contribution to the difficult relationship with their bosses.

There is a woman named Savannah, whom I have known forever. Savannah has long worked in corporate settings, and for some reason continues to work for the "biggest idiot" on the planet. When she took the job with idiot number one, I felt bad for her. Sometimes a bad apple shows up in a bushel. Then she would start to lose jobs, and within weeks of getting a new job, the next boss would be identified as also being from Idiot Island. Was she just a bad picker of jobs? Hard to say, but she's always quick to complain. In her words, the boss always seems to be intimidated by her, is heartless because he or she doesn't understand why she needs to take so much personal time, and is a total jerk if he doesn't close the office for at least two weeks over the holidays so she can do her Christmas shopping. Huh? In what reality does this make sense? News flash, Savannah! You do not intimidate the boss. Instead, he or she has to micromanage because you think just showing up by 10 a.m. for work is good enough. He also doesn't understand why you have to schedule seventeen doctors' appointments a week when you aren't nine months pregnant. No; in fact, the office should not be closed for two weeks around Christmas in spite of your need to hit the sales, brew cider, and giftwrap. Welcome to the real world.

Those women who are quick to point fingers and play victim at work are also the ones who aren't being the architects of their own lives. I've met women who enjoy being the victim. You see, as victims, they always have an excuse. Sure, bad stuff happens to all of us, but that doesn't mean you have to run around with the victim sign hanging from your neck. Being the architect of your life takes personal responsibility. It requires that you understand what you are good at, what you aren't, what you will tolerate, and what is going to make you incredibly happy. Being a single woman, perhaps bitter from a divorce and angry that you have to work at an outside job instead of stay home and bake cookies all day, is not the fault of your boss. You have allowed your architect to be silenced, and instead, are letting life live you. If you find yourself suddenly pointing the fingers at everyone but yourself, it's time for some self-reflection. I concede there are some bad bosses in the world. But more than likely, you're just a bad employee, and that speaks volumes about your being in the wrong job. If you find yourself in this position, where everything about your work begins to irritate you and you see more fault in others than yourself, it's time to have an internal heart-to-heart. The universe is trying to tap you on the shoulder and say, "Hello ... let's stop blaming and start doing ..." Your architect is telling you that you are standing in your own way. You are the square peg in the round hole, not your boss. It's time to listen.

Shortly after joining the law firm, I started a relationship with Colin. He and I had been pub friends for years. Given my love of England, it is no surprise that I would spend a lot of time at one of the English pubs in San Diego. My initial attraction to Colin was his sense of humor. He's tall, shaves his head, and walks with a bit of a swagger that is either confidence or the impression of it. To this day, he remains one of the funniest people I have ever known, and he has made me belly laugh more times than I can count.

At the beginning of our relationship, Colin was diagnosed with cancer. He was playing soccer one day and when he kicked the ball, his spine essentially folded up like an accordion. Unknown to him, a tumor on his spine had exploded, and my lovable Humpty Dumpty collapsed onto the field. Tests showed he was not only suffering from a broken back, but also a form of cancer that is usually found in older African-American men, neither of which comprise Colin's profile. To complicate the situation even more, Colin decided to leave his wife within months of coming out of the hospital. I had a knock on my apartment door one afternoon, and found Colin standing on my doorstep, telling me that he had left his wife, he was moving out, and he wanted to spend whatever time he had left with me. He asked me if he could die in my arms. If that doesn't knock you over, I don't know what will!

Colin and I were ultimately in a relationship together for more than three years. During that time we would live in three-month chapters, which were bookended by his doctors' appointments. Every three months he would have blood tests, and then we would visit the doctor for his results. Without even paying attention to the date of the next appointment, I could sense that one was coming up because his mood would change drastically, and our arguments would get more frequent. I soon realized that it was really the anxiety of the next doctor's appointment that was causing our friction. Or so I tried to convince myself. Starting a relationship with a man who had a cancer diagnosis and a divorce settlement was challenging enough. In addition, my closeness with my familial tribe and my unhappy career situation didn't really provide the best recipe for our success.

We broke up and put our three-year relationship back together more times than I can remember. In the song "You Don't Bring Me Flowers," by Neil Diamond and Barbra Streisand, there is a line: "And baby, I remember all the things you taught me; I learned how to laugh; and I learned how to cry; well, I learned how to love, even learned how to lie." When I was growing up, that song blared loudly from the tape deck of my mom's blue Datsun B210. My sister and I would take turns singing the male and female parts. Even now when it comes on the radio, I still ask her which part she wants to sing. This song summed up my relationship with Colin perfectly. About 90 percent of the time, Colin and I did a lot of laughing. But the 10 percent of our time together when there were tears, a lack of trust, and name-calling was emotionally draining and incapacitating. My parents have been married forty-five years, and I can count on one hand the number of times that they have argued. It was just never something we heard in our house. Instead, we still see them trust each other, encourage each other to have personal hobbies and other friends, and to be great partners to each other. Never once have I heard my dad use the C-word with my mom, nor has he called her a fat bitch. Clearly, Colin and I grew up in different homes. Learning how to argue is something I took away from my relationship, as well as the insight that you never know what is going on behind closed doors. We used to have knock-down-and-drag-outs in the car on the way to an event, and then walk in together like all was fine. For reasons I will never understand, Colin can be incredibly hurtful with his words. For the record, he *never once* hit me or caused me any physical harm, but I allowed him to say things to me that were disgusting and despicable. If that behavior happened once, shame on him. If I allowed that behavior for three years, then shame on me! If a girlfriend of mine were to tell me the same story about her boyfriend, I would claw his eyes out if he ever spoke to her that way. Yet, in my house, under the roof I was paying for from money I was making at a job I didn't love, I allowed a man to treat me less than I deserved. Um, hello … apparently I had fired the architect of my life!

In the wrong relationship and the wrong career, I was just treading water. I was trying to balance the snide comments between Colin and my family (both sides felt I was always siding with the other) and trying to find the independent Nicole deep down inside, who deserved to be in a relationship that did not cause her such stress. The kicker was when my nephew Ian, who would have been about six years old at the time, asked my sister, "Why does Colin always make Titi cry?" If you need to hold up a mirror of honesty, look no further than children.

I'm not trying to come across as being perfect in the relationship I had with Colin. He probably recalls our time together differently. I know it takes a certain man to fit into the tribe of my family. We are incredibly close, and there is an obligation that you will show up for every family event, which also includes Sunday dinners at my parents' house. The last few months Colin and I were together, his absence was noticed. At some point you just run out of energy to fight anymore, so you just move into management. I knew how to manage my relationship with him. I knew what would set him off and how I had to approach him about expectations I had for him to show up. You would think that a relationship that started with a cancer diagnosis, his divorce, and my family obligations would not be able to face anything else. In spite of all that, though, what really broke up Colin and me after three years was a lack of trust.

Remember in the movie *When Harry Met Sally*, when Billy Crystal's character announces that men and women can't really ever be friends without sex getting in the way? Colin truly believed that, and I did everything in my power to challenge his belief. Just shortly before I found myself in a formal relationship with Colin, I met a man named

Jack. There is plenty to say about my relationship with Jack, which you will read in future chapters. However, for the sake of being the architect of my life, I caved and let Colin dictate whom I could have as a friend. Shame on me.

My relationship with Colin became like a heavy trench coat that I could never take off. It weighed me down, and I eventually became another version of myself. I wish I had a dollar for every time I heard someone say, "What happened to the old Nicole?" or "Why doesn't she laugh anymore?" or my favorite, "Is she happy?" The answers were easy: The old Nicole had allowed her lack of self-esteem to permit herself to be treated worse than she deserved. She didn't laugh anymore because she was so beaten down emotionally that she couldn't find the strength. No; in fact, she wasn't happy. But for too long, I had convinced myself that the devil I knew, was better than the devil I didn't, and so I stayed. Sure Colin and I had plenty of laughs together, and when my family or friendship with Jack wasn't causing any grief, we had a lot of fun. But day in and day out, I was going through the motions and just letting life live me.

What I did learn in my relationship with Colin—besides the skill of arguing—was a new appreciation for what goes on in other people's homes. From the outside, it's easy to see the Stepford lives of your friends, but perception and reality live in two very different neighborhoods. Sadly, when I do share my story now, I often hear that a woman has allowed herself to be in a similar relationship, and all too often these women are super-successful, independent women who you would never guess are going home to men who call them everything under the sun. I'm fascinated—by my own story as well—that we as women allow that to happen. How can we be so independent in some areas of our lives and so subservient in others? How do we allow ourselves to get to a place of being called the "See You Next Tuesday" word and not immediately run for the hills? I had become so afraid of not having Colin that I chose not to get out until we were three years into our relationship.

What I am delighted to hear when I talk to other women who have had similar relationships is that there was a day when they just couldn't do it anymore, and they finally put an end to it. I'm driven by the feelings in my gut. Even though it causes so much frustration to someone totally different, like my sister, I can't make a move on something until I feel it in my gut. It just has to feel right. I'm not stubborn or expecting that it all has to go my way, but I will drag my feet until my stomach and my head are aligned. This is not a trait that benefits those being in the wrong relationship! It also contradicts my High D personality, but living in fear in a relationship put a muzzle on my self-worth. I was being dominated rather than dominating my own life.

Although my head was telling me that I was in the wrong place, my heart and my gut weren't yet in alignment, and so I stayed much longer than I ever should have. A part of me wondered, *If I just love him more, will he choose nicer words when we argue, or will he eventually want to be part of the familial tribe?* I really struggled with getting out of the relationship because of his illness. Who leaves a cancer patient to go to his three-month checkups on his own? I was raised to be committed and to love completely. I tried. I really tried.

The breaking point for us came around Easter. My family always has a big Easter feast, including a very competitive egg hunt and egg toss. Because my family celebrates everything, including the goldfish's birthday, it will come as no shock that there is an all-hands-on-deck call out when another holiday comes around. Because Colin's family do not celebrate Easter, and his parents often travel to their second home on the river for long weekends, I assumed we would spend the holiday with my family, but Colin felt differently. After weeks of us fighting about our relationship and trying to figure out how to keep it together, Colin informed me that he would not be coming to our Easter gathering. This left me without an egg-toss partner, which did not impress my competitive side. Something changed on that day, and my heart, head, and gut all seemed to move into alignment. I knew this was going to be the beginning of the end. What felt different this time was the fact that I was driving the decision. I had finally awakened the architect within me, and we were starting to design our exit strategy. Instead of fighting, I told him I would see him the next day.

By this time, he had lost his privilege of having keys to my house because he decided one day to conduct a Google search through my email. As a result, he found some emails between Jack and me from a time well before Colin and I were officially together. Imagine my surprise when I returned home from an alumni weekend up at UC Davis for an alumni event, and he decided to bombard me with emails from days past. I told him that he was no longer welcome in my home, and that he had to leave the keys. He did, and for days I assumed we would break up. Then he threatened to hurt Jack, and I did the only thing I knew how to do. I apologized. I put the relationship back together, and I became the "good girl" once again rather than the independent woman who should not have been intimated by a baseless threat. His bark was always bigger than his bite.

The day after Easter, Colin called me like nothing had happened. I tried to make small talk, but then my inner voice decided it was time to speak. Without controlling the words that came out of my mouth, I boldly stated, "I can't do this anymore." It didn't make sense to him.

He asked me, "What are you saying?" and then the floodgates opened.

But this time there were very few tears. Instead, what came flooding out was strength. "I'm sorry," I said, "you don't want to spend time and holidays with my family, but I do, and from this point forward I will always choose them over a man that has called me a bitch too many times to remember." I went on to say that I was tired of being ping-ponged between him and my family. I was no longer going to apologize for my friendship with Jack, and I wasn't going to be in a relationship that was not built on trust. I kept talking, and the more I said, the more I found my resolve. My architect was once again waving the flag of strength. She was tired of being cast aside by the meek and afraid Nicole, so she whispered in my ear, "I got this ..." and she found a way out for me.

Finally, I became my own champion, and I decided enough was enough. On April 8, 2007, I officially ended my relationship with Colin, and I started to design the next chapter of my life. For weeks, he thought I was kidding, and I would eventually snap out of whatever moment I was having. It's now been six years since we broke up. I wasn't kidding; when you are done, you are done!

Oh, and three months later, almost to the day, I gave notice at my job at the law firm. Who's your architect now?

Ask Yourself

Are you the architect of your own life?

What would you do right now if you knew you would not fail?

What is within your power to change today that will help you get one step closer to the life you want?

What are three areas of your life you feel could use improvement?

Ask three friends or co-workers what they would consider the top three qualities they like about you.

Identify how you could use your top three qualities and give them over to your inner architect to work on while you read the rest of the book.

CHAPTER TWO

What Is Keeping You Locked Up?

It's not who you are that holds you back,
it's who you think you're not.
—Author Unknown

SELF-DOUBT IS A FUNNY THING. FOR SOME REASON, we allow doubt or anxiety to become the internal voice that speaks louder than anything else. Like a lot of women, I can at times overthink just about everything. As someone who lives life at the direction of her head, heart, and gut, the voices in my head can be on Shuffle. My dad has often commented that my sister and I hold on to things for far too long, put way too much thought into most things, and worry far too much about what others are thinking and saying. Mars, meet Venus!

What is keeping you locked up? What is the story that you are telling yourself that doesn't allow you the permission to design your best life? Perhaps it stems from childhood, or an ex telling you that you are less than, or comparing yourself to Photoshopped women in magazines. It's easy to feel inferior when you are trying to keep up with the Joneses. Here's what age and wisdom have taught me: No one really cares about your story. Big disclaimer: I'm not saying that you aren't important or that people don't generally care about or are unconcerned about your life. But what I have found is that the story we so often hold onto as our shame is usually insignificant to most people.

Think of the last person you knew who was getting a divorce. You may have been concerned about that person's happiness and well-being, but in reality your life went on and you probably gave very little thought to the situation. But to the person who is actually getting a divorce, the situation is all-consuming, and the unfortunate one wonders what everyone will think. "What will my friends say?" The truth is, not much. People's lives move along, and they don't spend a whole lot of energy thinking of you as their divorced friend. You are just Mary or Bill, who happens to be divorced. But for Mary or Bill, this new state of life becomes a head case that questions one's place in the family, the community, or at the office. We are so quick to judge and shame ourselves for making a mistake, ending a relationship, or getting fired. Nobody cares—at least not on the emotional level you think they do.

In the interest of full -disclosure, I admit I have had plenty of scenes running through my head. This has caused me lots of self-doubt keeping me from using that same energy to move forward. As my dad has said, I can hold onto things, not because I'm holding a grudge, but because I'm not yet done processing. Embarrassingly, I have held onto something that ventures back all the way to my high-school prom.

I graduated in 1991 from high school. I was a varsity soccer and field hockey player and active in the student government. I was appointed to be prom coordinator, which was only a foreshadowing of what my career would ultimately become. It's no shock that I would eventually open an event management company. Events have been in my blood forever.

Although I excelled in sports and student government, I was shy when it came to boys. A special boy by the name of Daniel took an interest in me, and we became good friends. Daniel was tall and strong and had a mop of brown hair. He was the smarty-pants of our class. Today he is literally trying to cure cancer; he's that smart. He asked me to the ASB ball, and I asked him to the Sadie Hawkins dance. When he dedicated an ode to me in our advanced placement English literature class, I was convinced that we were headed toward being prom dates. I waited for the *big ask* to come. Unfortunately for me, the big ask came to my friend Stacy. For reasons I still don't fully comprehend, Daniel asked my very good friend Stacy to the prom. Wow! I certainly didn't see that coming. Disappointed that my shoo-in date was now not an option, I started to panic. I was also showered with self-doubt caused by my disbelief that I didn't get asked to the prom. Without Daniel, I didn't have another option for a date. How could the prom coordinator not have a date to the prom she was coordinating? Oh, the horror! I considered flying in my only male cousin, who is about my age. If he was from out of town, no one had to know that we were cousins, right? I could just tell everyone it was my long-distance boyfriend and feel very progressive. As the days ticked off and the prom was only weeks away, I was in a sheer panic and feeling more like the ugly duckling than ever before.

My good friend Marshall was our senior class president. I remember lamenting to him one day about my lack of a prom date. We started to create a list of possible dates, but no one seemed to be the right fit. Looking back now, this situation felt like a precursor to match.com. A few days later, Marshall's best friend, Mike, asked if he could speak to me. I knew Mike had a girlfriend, who was already away at college, so I assumed he just wanted information about the prom festivities. To my surprise, he asked if I wanted to go to prom with him. What was I hearing? A very pleasant, dark-haired, handsome, and overtly charming boy was actually asking me to prom? I could hear the angels singing from above! Ta-da! Of course I said yes in about three microseconds. Problem solved. But then I remembered he had a girlfriend, so of course I shyly asked why she wasn't going to be his date. He said she was already away at school and didn't want to go. Green light—her lack of interest was my blessing!

Mike could not have been the more perfect date. He rented a convertible for us instead of taking a limo. He took me to one of the nicest restaurants in San Diego, and then we enjoyed the (platonic!) after-party at a hotel with a group of friends. I couldn't feel more like a supermodel in my custom self-designed dress. My prom dress was a bright blue, three-quarter length, satin beauty with oversized shoulders and a sequined waistline. The tailor executed my design to perfection. No one is claiming it was a good design, but the tailor did the best he could. Back in 1991, I was right on point! If you went to school in the 1990s, you will agree that no prom was complete without shoes dyed to match your dress. I wore those bright blue-dyed satin pumps with style. I was bringing 1990s sexy back in more ways than one!

A few weeks after prom, Mike and I graduated and basically lost touch. One day, I was sharing prom stories with my college roommates when it suddenly hit me: Mike asked me to the prom as a charity date. This is when I pushed Record on the MP3 in my head. I concocted a story that went like this:

After Marshall heard my sob story about not having a date to prom, he acted as a good friend when he asked Mike if he would consider taking me. Although he had a girlfriend, Mike decided to work on his "getting into heaven" points, and he told the smoking-hot girlfriend that the pathetic prom coordinator didn't have a date, so Marshall asked him if he could take me. He didn't want to. Of course, he would rather have taken his college-bound girlfriend, but he was going to be a nice guy and do Marshall a favor. He was going to help the ugly duckling turn into a swan that night. In his mind, it was just one night he had to endure, so he would muster up the strength to do it.

For twenty years, I convinced myself of this story, and felt profoundly pathetic when I would recount my prom night. I always started by praising Mike for his generosity—assuming, of course, that he went on to run a charitable organization because he was such a giver. This was clearly demonstrated by his good deed for me.

In 2011, the class of 1991 celebrated our twentieth high school reunion. For the record, no, I did not coordinate it! To my delight, I saw Mike standing across the room when I arrived. This was my big chance for the ugly duckling to finally thank the brave boy who took me to prom. Mike couldn't have been lovelier when we connected, and I had the fortune of meeting his beautiful wife, Ana. She was very gracious to say that she was excited to meet Mike's prom date. I sunk a little, only imagining what stories she heard from his perspective.

After the typical reunion list of questions we all ask each other, I found my opportunity to finally get real with Mike. I started by saying, "I know I owe you a huge thank-you." He was perplexed by my comment. I went on to explain, "I know that you did me a huge favor by taking me to prom. I realize you had a girlfriend, so I'm not sure what you had to tell her so that she didn't get mad because you were taking me. For that reason, I just wanted to say thank-you. I know I was a charity date, and it probably put you in a difficult situation with her. I've waited twenty years to say thank-you and to tell you I know the real story. You're a noble guy."

Mike looked at me like I had six heads. He said, "I have no idea what you're talking about. My girlfriend and I had broken up, and she was certainly not interested in coming back to high school to go to the prom since she was already in college. I was feeling panicked that I wouldn't have a date, and then I realized that this great girl, who was cute and super-fun, was available, and I was honored to take you. If anything, I was sorry we weren't able to spend more time together at the dance because you were so busy coordinating the event."

After twenty years, at that very moment, I was able to push Eject on the crazy tape I had been playing in my head. For over two decades, I allowed self-doubt and a ridiculous feeling of being inferior and unwanted, to cloud my courage. There has always been a voice in my head that questioned if a man was really interested in me, or if I was still a charity case. This was absolutely not the fault of Mike. Instead, I made a huge assumption, and so I allowed the tape in my head to play louder than any other song in my life.

When I told my dad the story of seeing Mike again and making my confession, his response was, "Good, can we get off Fantasy Island now and start living again?" My dad knows all too well that my shy, unconfident, and vulnerable side was given way too much energy. Mike's comments to me at our twentieth high-school reunion became the permission I needed to cut the tape and to move on. You never know where permission will come from, but when it appears, grab on to it with both hands, and ride the wave.

As I travel around speaking to groups or talking to my own students, I often hear their stories. What I've come to learn is that usually the crazy story we are telling ourselves is far from reality. They tell me their fears, they tell me their ifs, ands, and buts, but they rarely tell me a story that isn't stemming from some tape in their own head. We have to learn how to stop competing with ourselves. That has been a battle for me over time, but I've come to realize that the amount of energy it takes to keep the hamster on the wheel in my head running non-stop is wasted. It gets me nowhere and all that running makes the hamster hungry.

I wonder if this new wave of successful CEO women who are pontificating about the need for women to "lean in" or "lean out" at work is really serving all women well. Although I agree with Sheryl Sandberg, the Chief Operating Officer of Facebook, in her recent book, Lean In, when she stresses the importance of women designing the lives they want professionally, I do think her message is limiting in the sense it is aligned more closely to women wanting a corporate career. I will however agree that until there is a parenting shift in the home, with more men getting engaged and taking responsibility for issues with childrearing, the shift to women leaning in at the boardroom table is potentially mute.

Unless you are making well over seven figures, have the million-dollar nursery next to your office, and have a staff of people running your home and life, it's a little hard to get behind the leaning in. Most women can't afford to "lean in" the way corporate America is structured today.

What if you don't want to be the woman who makes it to the corner office? Or what if you are a woman who has no interest in having children? Or what if you want to be the woman who wants to succeed in her life and have children? How loud must the voices in her head be as she tries to become Wonder Woman in all areas of her life? Enough! Stop competing with the person everyone expects you to be and start creating the woman (or man) you want to become. In future chapters, we are going to talk about ways you can start to design the life you want to live, but first you have to cut the tape and unlock yourself!

As the owner of The Henley Company, an event, travel, and lifestyle concierge firm, I, along with my staff, have the pleasure of working with busy executives and their families. As their personal concierges, we manage their busy lives, while giving them the gift of time. We manage their to-do list so they can focus their energy on enjoying life. We believe that recess is not just a concept that elementary school children should enjoy, so I created a company focused on unique experiences, travel opportunities, and special events for our clients.

We had the opportunity to be of service to a very busy executive woman, whom we shall call Jane. When I met Jane, her very first words to me were, "I need you; I'm so overwhelmed!" We always like when our clients understand the value of their time, so we were excited to help Jane bring order to her busy life. When I met with her at her home, we talked about her greatest needs and current list of projects. For a few months, Jane was on a monthly retainer with us. We would check in with her regularly and would manage any requests she had. But then the requests started to get less frequent. When I reached out to her to check on her satisfaction with our services, her response was: "Your level of service is great. I just don't know how to ask someone to help me to manage my life. I'm not comfortable delegating my needs." When I told her that it's not uncommon for women to feel like they have to juggle all the balls, she agreed.

I have now been in business for over six years. During that time, I have had the great fortune of working with a diverse group of corporate clients and busy individuals. Recently, I took a few minutes to look back over a list of my current concierge clients. Only three current clients are female. Although I've made an effort to reach out, I have learned that women are still not comfortable asking for help. It's rare that I meet a woman who isn't intrigued by what I do for a living. Nine times out of ten, the next comment out of her mouth is, "I could so use your services! You are like having a wife!" With common courtesy, I laugh, but in the back of my mind, I know she will never call.

For some reason, the thought of juggling the demands of work, home, and family still makes a woman feel noble. Even though she might feel harried, overwhelmed, and underappreciated, a woman would rather expend all of her energy looking like a superhero. I'm fascinated by this philosophy. Now before you start shouting at the book that there is no way I can make that sweeping statement because I'm not a mother, just settle yourself down. I admit that not having birthed a miracle from my loins, it's hard for me to understand the demands that being a mama bear puts on women, but that doesn't mean I can't observe what is happening in society. I'm surrounded by a lot of fabulous women who have earned the title of mother. I watch the struggle; I hear them use words like "mama guilt," and I'm fascinated when women make comments like the receptionist at my dentist's office once told me, "I want to work out, but I would feel bad if I was taking that time away from my child." Isn't there a reason the airlines tell us to put our own masks on before anyone else's in the event of an emergency? If we can't take care of ourselves, we are of little service to others.

Personal concierge services are far more reasonably priced than most people think. However, it's the notion of hiring someone to do your grocery shopping, book your travel, or take your car for an oil change that seems to make women itchy. It's really not the cost of the services they struggle with; it's the tape in their heads that has not given them permission to allow someone else to take care of them. They wonder, "What might the other women in the neighborhood think if I didn't do everything?" Oh the horror, if they were to spot me taking a yoga class while my concierge is turning my to-do list into a done list! What's wrong with us leaning on each other for help? For so long, we have played the role of nurturers, but women are not comfortable with being nurtured. Our genetic makeup and history have seen to it.

How many times have we said to someone, "Call me if you need anything," but the person never does? Perhaps we say it with a hope that he or she won't actually call. Why is it so hard for us to ask for help or actually take up the offer for help? Hillary Clinton became famous for saying that, "It takes a village to raise children." Wouldn't it be great if we took that to heart and actually lived like villagers?

When a woman tells me that she couldn't possibly afford to hire a concierge (which really means she hasn't given herself permission to ask for help), my standard response is, "Then I hope you will consider creating a concierge circle in your community." That often gets a perplexed look. By definition, the word *concierge* means the keeper of the keys and candles. Centuries ago, it was that person's job to meet the traveling noblemen and to be their go-to person while these men were paying a visit to their comrades. The concierge was the helper in the castle. Couldn't you use a helper?

Let's Start Leaning "On" Each Other
Rather Than Leaning "In" or "Out"

Think about how powerful it would be if a community of women started to co-op their lives. If Betty is going to the market on Monday, why couldn't she put out the word to see if anyone needed anything? If you were making a run to Target, why would you not ask if you could pick up something for your neighbor? Let's start leaning "on" each other versus singularly leaning "in." I've heard from several of my friends with small children that they are starting to run cooperative summer camp programs where one mom takes a day when she is responsible for the entertainment or activity of the other five to seven kids. On this day, the other moms get a day to themselves to spend however they want. Instead of thinking about five days worth of activities for their kids, now the moms have to think about only one. They share the burden and are helpers to each other. This concept seems brilliant to me.

There is power in the community. Raising the children, sharing responsibilities, and spreading the workload have led to healthier, happier moms. But what is most important is that these moms have stopped competing for the title of supermom. They start by ejecting the tape in their heads that they have to do it all.

Permission to silence the voices in your head—granted!

Ask Yourself

What is keeping you locked up?

What is the tape in your head saying?

Do you have a concierge circle? If so, who can you lean on? If not, who in your life could you invite into your concierge circle?

What do you need the most help with? How can your concierge circle give you the most support?

CHAPTER THREE
Being Done and Letting Go

I fall so hard inside the idea of you.
That's why you can't say what I mean.
Wanna stay but I think I'm getting outta here.
I fall so hard inside the idea of you.
— Dave Matthews Band, "The Idea of You"

I GUESS I ALWAYS THOUGHT THAT I WOULD EASE INTO adulthood. Somehow the feeling would come as the birthdays ticked off and innocence transitioned into maturity. I certainly never thought maturity would all come in a moment. There have been milestones in my life that on the surface would equate to being a "grown-up," but even in those experiences I somehow hung onto my youth and ability to separate myself from the "adults" in the room. This is not to say that I wasn't a fully functional, card-carrying member of adulthood. I guess I had just not yet chosen to fully embrace everything it meant, especially with matters of the heart. Instead, like Rod Stewart suggested, I just wanted to be "Forever Young."

I thought for sure I would feel grown-up when I graduated with a master's degree and soon boarded a plane to live in a foreign country. That seemed like a grown-up thing to do, but that didn't trigger the feeling. Then I thought surely it would be when I took the fancy law firm job, earned the hefty paycheck, and bought a BMW. These all seemed like grown-up acts on the surface, yet they didn't trigger the feeling either. Maybe it would be when I was talking to the loan officer over the phone, and he told me that I qualified for my first home purchase without my parents needing to cosign; that was certainly a big moment, but still the feeling didn't come. And then I was confident the feeling would come when I walked away from the big job in corporate America three months after I told the boyfriend with cancer that it was over between us. I also thought the feeling of maturity would come when I ventured into self-employment. Somehow, even with all that change, it didn't matter. Life clicked on day after day, and I continued to be the hamster on the wheel in my protective bubble of youth.

The Prince Is Not Always Charming

So imagine the impact I felt when on a Saturday night in April of 2008, I officially became a grown-up, and I started living the cliché of "What doesn't kill you makes you stronger." I was thirty-four, and life as I knew it was soon going to be over. Dealing with the grown-up stuff didn't evolve over time; instead, it presented itself in the flash of an eye, like the stories you hear of people crossing the road and not seeing the semi truck that ran them over. Well, my truck—the one that got me—surely had all eighteen wheels, and in every word I heard that changed my life, I felt the tires individually run over me. I can push Play in my head at any given moment to this day and completely relive what happened that night: where Jack and I both stood, what we were wearing (he had on red, plaid, flannel pajama bottoms and a white T-shirt, and I had on jeans and a black and white-striped fitted tee under a black cardigan) and what I was doing.

You see, I was standing in his kitchen cutting mushrooms when he finally stopped pacing and started talking. I lifted my head to look him in the eye, when he nervously sat down in front of me on the other side of the kitchen counter. Then, I instantly got a rush of women's intuition that told me nothing was ever going to be the same.

Quietly, he said, "Someone's having a baby, and I've been told I could be the father." As quickly as our eyes had met, I suddenly turned my head and looked down because I wanted to know if I was still cutting the mushrooms, or if it was truly my own heart that had just been sliced open. A baby? It *could* be yours? The questions started swirling in my head. This was the man I had convinced myself was the greatest love of my life; he was my soul mate. He was the one that fueled my passion for life, for my work, for making a difference. His friendship was what I had fought for with the cancer patient, and it ultimately cost me my relationship with a man who wholeheartedly loved me. He was the one … the only one … he was my best friend … he was my Prince Charming. He was also the one looked me in the eye and said point blank, "No, there isn't anyone else." He was the one who told me he loved me over and over and over again. And looking back now, I guess that was enough for me, so I didn't force him to ever commit the relationship into anything more than being "best friends" with benefits. Maybe that was my fear of losing what I had with him. Regardless of what life had thrown at us, we always clawed our way back to each other, and he promised me we always would.

I knew Jack was "the one" the night I first met him five years before. It was a moment that Hollywood directors try to recreate on the big screen. It was that moment where you come face-to-face with someone that you have never met before, and you know that your life will never be the same. That's what happened to us. Jack ran past me on the indoor soccer field as I was warming up for our game. My co-ed team had fallen short of male players that night, and Jack asked if he could play. I looked up as I was tying my shoes, and I was stopped in my tracks. I've always thought that he resembles Matthew McConaughey with his piercing blue eyes and a cheeky look that could melt your clothes right off of you. He was athletic, brilliant, and an unbelievably good, fun-loving friend. He lived without rules and challenged the system. This had made him both financially successful and a loner by choice. His dysfunctional childhood was fascinating to me and completely opposite from the suburban bubble I grew up in. You either loved him or dismissed him when you first met him. On more than one occasion, he confessed to me that drinking was the escape mechanism he needed and the excuse he always had to draw upon. Yet despite all of that, I was in love the moment I saw him, and my life indeed never was the same. In just one night on that soccer field, he had worked his way into my head and heart. From that night, we started to play not only the game together on the field, but in life as well. He was unique, incredibly special, and he made me feel significant. I had finally met my match.

If Facebook needed a definition of the "It's Complicated" relationship status, we could have been the poster children for it. Nothing about our friendship, relationship, or any other label you wanted to put on it made sense to anyone but him and me. We were both in relationships with other people when our planets collided, but we both knew that night that our meeting was the beginning of something significant that could never be defined by anyone but the two of us.

Before this fateful night in his kitchen, Jack and I had been friends for almost five years. In the last year, we were officially unattached and not in relationships with other people, or so I thought. When I told him I was no longer in a relationship with Colin, that situation gave us room to be friends once again. That's when we picked up immediately where we had left off. While I was dating Colin, Jack had decided that it was too complicated for us to have a friendship. It was causing me too much angst because of Colin's jealousy, and Jack didn't want to be the cause of any trouble. At the time, I was heartbroken that he thought we shouldn't be friends anymore, but then I realized that it was a great gift of friendship. Out of love for me, he got out of the way. That's how I would define love.

With a knife in my hand and a mound of mushrooms in front of me, suddenly I was in the kitchen with Jack sitting across from me. In an instant he was the one who forced me to step out of my bubble of innocence and into the reality of being a grown-up.

Needless to say, emotion flooded over my body as he sat quietly and looked at me. He wanted me to say something, but before I could even utter the words, I got really angry inside. Funnily enough, in that moment, the earthquake that had just happened had little to do with him and everything to do with the fairy tales I had been told as a young girl. I did what I was supposed to: I read the stories; I dressed up like the characters on Halloween; I read that I could be a princess and eventually I would meet my Prince Charming. But nowhere did I ever read that Prince Charming was going to tell me that he was having a baby with someone else. I wanted to run from the kitchen and to my nearest library to flip frantically through the books I had from my youth. Maybe I had missed a page or a chapter where the princess in the story suddenly went rogue and said, "Hey girls, that whole 'they lived happily ever after' thing really doesn't happen, take it from me. It's just a character the old guy who wrote the story asked me to play." Maybe that was in the special edition that we couldn't afford because everything we did as children required a coupon. Did I get the coupon version of the fairy tale? Because I didn't pay full price, did I not get the whole story?

In an instant, I suddenly wanted to rewrite the fairy tale to tell every little girl that comes after me, "You have to listen and know that sometimes the prince is not that charming." As I refocused on the man sitting in front of me, I finally had the courage to divert my eyes from the pool just outside the window and looked at his face. I took a breath and without emotion asked, "When did you start fucking other women?" And as if the concrete wrecking ball had not yet cracked every ounce of my youth, he leaned back in his chair, shook his head and said, "I can't believe you just made this moment about you."

I thought for sure that the next scene would be a hodgepodge of people moving chairs into a support group circle in the middle of the kitchen, and I was supposed to stand up and say, "Hello everyone, my name is Nicole and I am officially a grown-up."

Apparently he has a different version of the *Best Friends Handbook* he lives by. When I called him out on the lies he had continually told me, either it didn't resonate with him, or maybe he was activating his escape mechanism. I guess I must not have received that chapter of this book either. Blame it on another coupon! From his reaction to my question, it was obvious that what he was expecting me to do was to put the knife down, hurl myself over the kitchen counter, and embrace him into my bosom, while I stroked his head, told him I loved him, and would proudly stand by him as his life got completely turned upside down. I knew he could kiss his understanding of "normal" away. His look of disappointment in me could only match the disappointment that I felt in my heart.

I tried to regain my composure that night, and we tried to make our way through the salads in front of us, but there was really no point. I was torn about what to do. Everything in me was shouting to get my purse, run out the door, and never return to the man that had not only broken my heart, but had shattered the fairy tale. Ironically, every time I tried to get up, my feet would not move. Plenty of people in his life, starting with his parents, had abandoned him and been the cause of much disappointment. I loved him too much to be another name on that list. Even as I stood across from the man that I profoundly loved, yet was so disappointed in, I couldn't run. Instead, I did what I always do: I just hugged him and we cried together.

I hoped that somehow this would all go away and it would become something we would laugh about down the road over a few beers. The power of his hug back to me indicated he wished for the same. As the days turned into weeks and we waited for the results of the paternity tests, I even started praying and going to church in a futile attempt to beg God to make this a lesson and not an alteration to his life forever. I even went so far as to ask our family priest to put him on a prayer list.

I thought maybe Father Lonell would have an "in" with the big man upstairs, and he would help us get out of this situation. This was not to be. Maybe I should have put more money in the collection basket the years before.

What happened since that night became the ultimate test in unconditional love, not only for him, but also ultimately for me. There isn't a person in my inner circle who didn't question why I had not run as far away from him as I could during that difficult time. Telling my family and my friends felt impossible. Even though he was the one who had to say he was having a baby with a woman he barely knew, I felt like humiliation rained down on me every time I told someone else this soap opera story. My humiliation came from allowing myself to believe in the idea of what could have been. Everyone knew he was my world, and yet I wasn't even sure what planet I was living on anymore.

As we came to terms with the situation, our friendship certainly was tested. I tried to stay focused and to throw myself into work, but my mind was constantly distracted. He would try to use humor to diminish the severity of the situation, but there was always the baby elephant in the room. The late night phone calls asking me to come out for a play date continued. It felt like we needed each other more than ever before. He was humble but scared; I was sad but trying to be supportive. The safe space for both of us was always found in each other's company, enjoying a beer together, and talking about everything and anything under the sun.

During the pregnancy, I watched a successful, confident man, who had the great ability to keep everything under control, lose that control completely because of a baby in the womb, whom he befriended through sonograms. He realized he really knew nothing. I comforted a man who appeared to be strong and stoic, while he cried profoundly over the fear of what was happening. Through it all, he asked me to continue to fight for our friendship and love, and became even more vocal about introducing me as his best friend to everyone we met, including the baby's mama. As lovely as that sentiment sounded at the time, there was still a part of me that wanted to yell and scream and demand that he really hear the moment my heart broke. To be honest, I just wanted him to say he was truly sorry because he really was, not because he thought it was what I needed to hear. But when he told me that this situation had "nothing to do with me," he really told me that he had stopped listening, and I didn't matter.

I attempted to make him understand that my reaction to his statement was the result of years of lies that he told me. Still, I soon discovered that regarding this topic, anything I said was just noise to him. I believed him when he told me he loved me. I believed him when he told me there was no one else. I believed him, even on the night when his sperm met her egg, when he told me that he was happy with how things between us were, even though we were a complicated couple.

That's what you do when you love a man: you trust in what he says. For months, I would get a ping in my heart when he told me that I was his best friend, and he appreciated my unending support. But I would be less than truthful if I didn't wonder where *my* best friend was the night his forty-seven Bud Lights dictated the rest of our lives. Why did I have to be the only supporting cast member? If he really loved me and respected what we shared, we wouldn't have been in this position.

Unfortunately, that is not what the universe decided. In December of 2008, a beautiful, very innocent baby girl came into the world to two parents who agreed to be partners in parenting, but nothing else. Eventually, she will learn that a tremendous man, who has a profound ability to create a unique world around him, is raising her to live her best life. However, she will also learn that he has a lot of flaws. What she will probably never know is the depth of my love for her father. In fact, she will probably never even know I exist.

When I met Jack, he became the meter for measuring every other relationship against. Short of my father, Jack was one of the greatest men I've ever known. To say that I loved him with every ounce of my being is an understatement. There has been no man prior to or since who has ever made me feel as alive as I did when I was with Jack. We clicked. We loved each other. We battled, and then one day it was just over.

Prior to the baby's arrival, and for about a year after, we tried the best we could to hold our relationship together. I tried hard to be supportive and figured the innocent baby shouldn't feel my heartache, but it wasn't always easy. Jack adjusted to being a single dad, and admittedly, he did very well. The relationship with the baby's mother became hostile, as she grew to understand that their relationship would be nothing more than co-parents to a lucky little girl. I supported him in his efforts to craft a parenting agreement, and to always try to do the right thing. With all of the chaos, it was still my phone that would ring late at night, asking for me to come out to see him. We could then have another one of our endless conversations that were always philosophical and comical, to the background music of the Dave Matthews Band. To this day, whenever I hear a DMB song, the memory takes me back to Jack's house, and I have a slight tinge of the good old days. I admit, in my heart of hearts, I miss the man I thought was my friend.

And then our relationship really started to unravel. As much as I continued to defend him, and as much as those in my sphere questioned me as to why I would stay with a man who had caused me so much pain, Jack and I had a pact that we would always remain friends. Just you and me against the world, right kid? We promised one night that we will meet again at the age of ninety, in our rocking chairs on the porch to laugh and recount the stories of our lives. Funny what love will make you promise, isn't it?

With the depth of my love for Jack, I can honestly say that I gave that relationship everything I could offer. I've never felt the depth of passion, chemistry, and sheer bliss as I did the moment he stepped into my life. At the time, I thought Jack was the love of my life. I still have times when I ask if he might actually still be, even after all of the pain and suffering that relationship caused me in the end. He became my blessing and my curse. What I came to realize is that I loved the idea of him and everything he represented.

As Jack became accustomed to being a single father, I stood on the sidelines trying to be supportive. We consistently teetered between arguing and making up. I told him that I would rather fight with him than to make love with someone else. At the time, I believed it.

One night, Jack asked if I could babysit, and being such a good "friend," I said yes. I later learned that he asked me to babysit so he could take another girl out on a date. If that didn't make me feel even more used, little else could have. I had been so available, so accommodating, and so loving to Jack that he benefited from having his cake and eating it, too.

A week or so later, when he declared the latest fling was a little kooky, who do you think was standing right there, smirking that yet another girl tried to come between us and had failed?

For the next several months, we continued our dance of getting along famously and then getting on each other's nerves. My heart was still cracked, but I couldn't imagine my life without Jack, so I put up with anything and everything he tossed my way. I felt like he was always testing me and moving the bar, although he admitted that he didn't really allow me to get to know his entire self.

On several different occasions, he quietly said that it should have been the two of us having a baby. During those times, I couldn't help but wonder: If that was truly how he felt, why would he choose to have sex with a woman he knew only casually? Both times he said it, I waited for Bob Barker from *The Price Is Right* game show to come out of the closet and say, "Thanks for playing. We have some lovely parting gifts for you because you are the showcase runner-up." I said nothing when he made those comments because I couldn't decide if they were the most insensitive things he possibly could have said to me, or if they were his way of saying he was sorry. Either way, nothing changed. You are very right, my friend. This baby should have been ours, not because I trapped you, but because it would have truly been the product of a beautiful friendship. Unfortunately, that was not destined to be the story for us. Instead of his best friend having a baby with him, a woman he casually knew had given him the greatest gift of his life. You bet I felt like the runner-up.

Fast forward to August of 2011. The Dave Matthews Band was playing in San Diego. As we had done for years, Jack and I, together with a big group of friends, had tickets for the concert. Leading up to this day, we had been nagging at each other, but usually we could pick up where we left off previously, and the laughs would ensue. Something felt different that day. When I arrived at his house for a pre-concert barbecue, I found a house full of people and one almost incapacitated, very drunk Jack. It was only three in the afternoon. Shots of Captain Morgan and party boy Jack had been getting it on together since breakfast. Jack could be an asshole on the best of days, but with the liquid courage of both Bud Light and Captain Morgan, you never knew which personality you were going to get. He was the life of the party and had the endless credit card. (Of course, this made him popular at every bar he visited.) The bar crowd can always handle an asshole as long as he is buying the next round, and the one after that, and the one at last call.

As cars were loading up to caravan to the concert, a pretty blonde girl came through the door. Jack made some comment to her about the size of her boobs, and I turned to his sister and said, "He will fuck her before the end of the night." His sister tried to dismiss my comment with a "no way," but I just knew better. I had lived through his patterns already. Drunk and indestructible, Jack was on his way to see his idol, Dave Matthews. Jack was wearing his alcoholic armor that day, so no one would be able to get through to him when he was in that indignant mode. The latch on his escape mechanism had been pulled.

As we all walked to our cars, Jack pulled me aside and said, "You know I love you, right? Let's go have a great time tonight and promise to always be nice to each other." I agreed and we kissed.

When I met up with the group later at the concert, I found Jack and the blonde trying to out-drink each other over shots of Captain Morgan. As she fumbled for more money to buy the next round, I leaned over and asked her to not kill my friend that night. My biggest fear, along with his sister's, has always been that he won't wake up the next morning because of how much he drank the night before. Mister Indestructible needed to know that he had reached his limit. She didn't seem to realize the damage that had already been done. But then again, this new girl didn't seem to know much. She was a friend of a friend, so they had only just met that night. Of course, she didn't know who I was or the history we had shared. To her, I was just the old fuddy-duddy telling her to stop trying to kill her drinking buddy who was the life of the party.

As DMB took the stage, everything seemed fine. Jack was in his typical life-of-the-party mood, and the music flooded over us like the perfect safety net for our friendship. Everything is right in the world when Dave Matthews is involved, right? Actually, no.

A few songs in, I noticed that the blonde had made her way over to Jack's lap, and they were drunkenly fondling each other while they were sitting down. Um, hello, I'm standing right here!

Remember earlier when I talked about being the architect of your own life, and the day my inner architect opened her mouth and finally told Colin I was done? Well, she made a repeat performance. Up until now, only Santa Claus had worked fewer days than my own architect!

With a snap of my head, I called him out. I did so right there in front of all our friends, with Dave blasting away in the background, and the crowd going wild. I told him he was a pathetic excuse for a DMB fan, and he should be ashamed of himself for sitting down at a concert. It was a passive-aggressive way of telling him to stop making me feel like a fool. "Who's this fucking guy?" I asked. "Who is the guy who claims to be the biggest DMB fan, but is allowing some girl to keep him sitting down at this concert?"

We both knew I wasn't talking about the concert. She looked at me sheepishly, realizing that there was more history between Jack and me than she was aware of, and slowly she crawled off him. He stood up and walked over to me as all our friends laughed nervously. He put his arm around me and said the last thing he has ever said to me, "I know what you are doing. Stop being a fucking bitch."

There it was. That absolute defining moment when you realize that what has been will no longer be the normal anymore. In that moment, with the pure chaos of the concert around us, I knew that we were finished. I was done. I was tired of being in the way. Correction, I was tired of being in my *own* way. For far too long, I had convinced myself that Jack was worth everything, even at the expense of my own heart, happiness, and health. He said jump; I said how high. I was tired of jumping. My architect forbade me from jumping anymore and decided we were going to keep my feet planted firmly from this point forward. I then realized that there was no longer a point to making him a priority when he clearly had only ever considered me an option.

Drunken boy and blonde girl walked off together that night before the concert ended. Three weeks later, his sister told me he had asked Blondie to marry him and changed his Facebook status to "Engaged." Three months later she called again, this time to tell me that a justice of the peace married them. She cried when she told me, but said that I deserved to hear it firsthand. Jack's sister has more integrity and has earned more of my respect than her brother ever deserved. I've never heard from him since the moment they walked off together at the concert. The architect never made any effort to call him or to reengage. When you are done, you just know you are done.

All I can do now is think of him with fond memories and try to shower him with love and light from afar. I hope he finds the true happiness he deserves, and that he can find a purpose in his life beyond the bottom of a Bud Light bottle.

I'm grateful to have known him, learned from him, and loved him, and now I am grateful that chapter is closed. Correction: My anxiety is really grateful that relationship is over. I now know you can forever be in love with a person yet not like the current version of who they are. He will always hold a part of my soul; but our lives are now better served traveling our separate journeys.

The fairy tale might tell you that Prince Charming will one day sweep you off your feet, but the reality is that the fairy tale lives inside you. Regardless of the ugly stepsisters you meet, the witches who cast their spells, or the bad apples you have to eat, the fairy tale does have a happy ending. It might not be with the man you thought it would be, living in the castle on the hill, but where it ends is where you begin … to design the life you want to lead. Finally, with courage and faith in your heart, you start to design the life you want. It's almost like the fairy tale that once began "Once upon a time" now begins "To thine own self be true."

I champion the importance of having a small but mighty group of women around you when your world starts to crumble. What the fairy tale does get right is the notion of a knight in shining armor. Instead of being a handsome man, though, the "knights" are your girlfriends who serve as the cavalry you need when in battle. They are the ones that have told me they won't let me fail, and they are the ones who have promised to tell me the truth even when I don't want to hear it. If I don't like what they have to say, they are the ones who have promised to be in the same spot when I decide to come back to them. They will never tell me, "This has nothing to do with you." They are the ones who helped me to rewrite my own fairy tale by giving me the strength of their support. They are my real friends, and they are the characters that should be highlighted in every fairy tale.

Prince Charming, as much as I loved him, shattered my heart. Even though I now can value what that relationship has taught me, it is the girlfriends in my life who have shown their true character. They gave me the strength to give myself permission to get out and to get up when I was indeed crumpled.

If I have learned anything by crossing the threshold from childhood to adulthood, it is that you have to follow your own heart, and you have to let your feet dictate where you belong. Try as I might to run away from a flawed man, I couldn't for a very long time; our connection was far too strong, and I just wasn't ready. It took a while for my heart, head, and gut to get in alignment. This was not a futile attempt to try to hold onto the white picket fence, walking down the aisle and life with our 2.5 children, and a golden retriever. That fantasy vanished over a cutting board full of mushrooms. Instead, this whole situation taught me that you have to stand up for what you believe in. Ultimately, I believed in a life that no longer involves him. I could finally see life beyond Jack. I was done with this chapter of my life.

People are where they are in life, and there was nothing I could do to move him from loving me to being in love with me, if he didn't really feel it. I do believe in my heart of hearts that deep down he did love me, but he wasn't able to give me more than what he had. I couldn't love him enough to make him stop drinking; I couldn't love him enough to convince him not to sleep with other women; nor could I love him enough to stop him from marrying the blonde. But none of that matters now. I had to decide to love myself more than I could ever love him.

This is when I learned that being selfish is perfectly acceptable, and I gave myself permission to do just that. I thought Jack was the love of my life; I've realized that he was actually just the love of one chapter in my life.

There is a part of me that even thanks him for dragging me into adulthood because I realized that what innocence and youth were hiding from me all those years was my self-esteem. By becoming a grown-up, I can no longer hide behind a self-imposed self-esteem crisis and let life happen to me. Instead, I had to become my own superhero and put on my cape of hope that one day there will be a man worthy of my love. Such a man will cherish me and treat me like the princess all the stories told me I could become.

After years of tears, disappointment, and the challenge of unconditional love, I have also learned that fantasy and reality live in two different neighborhoods. Unfortunately, my town no longer had a Cinderfella as its mayor. That's okay. I've learned that I can self-govern, and so I have chosen to hang my new shingle: Welcome to My Grown-Up Town, Population 1. Permission to be done and let go: Granted!

Ask Yourself

What relationships are no longer serving you?

Are you allowing someone to be a priority while he or she is treating you like an option?

Whom do you consider to be your knight in shining armor?

Is there a situation in your life that should be moved to "done"?

CHAPTER FOUR

Who Is in Your Circle?

My biggest influences are strong, creative women that chart their
own path, lead their own lives, and drive the course of history.
—Rachael Ray

IT'S BEEN SAID THAT FRIENDS ARE THE FAMILY WE
choose. We are born into some relationships, but we choose most of
the people we spend time with. It's never been more important to
choose wisely. I think about the small but mighty group of people that
I have in my life outside of my family, and I am proud of whom I have
chosen. I'm not one who needs to have a phonebook full of contacts,
but rather a select few who are members of my go-to crowd. I have
lots of acquaintances and professional friends, but when it comes to
those I enjoy grabbing a drink with or really opening myself up to,
the number is rather low. This is perfectly acceptable to me. I am very
much a quality versus quantity person.

As you think about who is currently in your circle, is it time to do
a little housecleaning? I believe people come into our lives for a reason,
a season, or a lifetime. Colin and Jack were season ticket holders,
but now I've made room for someone else to love. All charming,
handsome and professionally motivated men should apply!

Who Do You Hang With—
Basement Dwellers or Penthouse Cheerleaders?

It's important to take regular inventory of the people you are surrounding yourself with on a fairly consistent basis. Whales aren't born with barnacles; the barnacles get stuck to them over time. Friends are the same way. Sometimes we just look up and realize that the people we have surrounded ourselves with are actually not serving us in a positive capacity. Are your friends basement dwellers or penthouse cheerleaders?

Basement dwellers are those who camp out on a negative island. They are the naysayers, the people who think they will never make anything of their lives. Basement buddies are negative about everything. They are the ones who become your man-haters because of a bad relationship; they think every boss is out to get them because they have been fired from more than one job; and they are never supportive of anyone who is making more of an effort to be successful than they are ever capable of. These are the parents who tell their children they will never amount to anything; the boyfriends who are emotionally abusive; and your friends who would be intimidated if you really lost those twenty-five pounds. We all have these dwellers in our lives, and somehow, instead of calling them out and setting them free to dwell somewhere else, we allow their voices to become our doubts. If you decide tomorrow that you want to sell everything and live in a mud hut in the middle of the Sahara Desert selling bracelets made out of twine, the basement dwellers will tell you it's too hot, you don't have the money, and you didn't pass home economics so you don't know how to braid.

In contrast, *penthouse cheerleaders* are those who are excited about every opportunity you present. Your cheerleaders are going to help you scour craigslist until you find the perfect mud hut to buy in the Sahara Desert; they are going to go with you to jewelry-making classes and will help you to find stylish zip-off pants that you'll need because of the heat. They will never tell you that you can't do something; instead, they are the encouragers. They know that even if you shoot for the moon and miss, the journey will be amazing, and you will have stars in your eyes.

Until I was in my thirties, I didn't really value my relationships with other women to the extent that I could have. When I was growing up, I was a bona fide tomboy, athletic and more comfortable sticking close to the nest than risking great adventures away from my family. My High D did rear its head at the age of seven when I was playing with our Australian shepherd in the front yard. Australian shepherds are known to have different-colored eyes, one blue and one brown. When the neighbor boy asked me why Scooter's eyes were different colors and started to make fun of her, I looked him straight in the eye and said, "If you ever make fun of my dog again, I'm going to rip your lips off." My parents had to apologize to his mom and dad. I was completely wrapped up in the apron strings of my familial home and would defend them to the death, even the dog. Because of the closeness of my family, I would rely more on this nuclear unit than outside friends. I had plenty of friends, don't get me wrong; but my circle of best friends was small. It was when life started to throw curveballs at me (um ... hello—he's having a baby with someone else) that I started to find the true value in my girlfriends and began to understand how significant they are to my circle.

Funny as this might sound coming from a woman in her late thirties, I think a lot of my self-doubt came at the hands of a six-year-old in the clothing department at Target when I was eighteen years old. I remember shopping one day in the women's department, and this adorable little brown-haired girl in a pink long-sleeve shirt and blue leggings came out from under one of the dress rounders. She caught me off guard, and I sort of laughed when I said hello to her, expecting that she would giggle and run off with her bouncing pigtails. She stopped as she stood next to the dresses, from which she had just come underneath, and she looked me dead in the eye and said, "You are the ugliest woman I have ever seen." Telling this story is not easy for me because on one level I feel horribly pathetic and ridiculous. As a teenager, the comment of a six-year-old wounded me not only then, but also for decades to come. Link that with my prom date debacle, my lack of boyfriends, and an overactive imagination telling me that I was never good enough, and that experience in Target became a defining moment. The less I allowed myself to be courted by boys (poor Jacob Drange tried to kiss me at Aquarius skating rink when we were twelve, and I was overcome with such anxiety that I had to call my mom immediately to come get me), the further I isolated myself from them and allowed myself to believe that the words the young girl spoke must have been true.

The less I felt included, the more I was convinced that I was a leper and no one would want Dragon Face. Instead of turning to my girlfriends, I retreated. Remember, it was one of my best friends who said yes to Daniel 's invitation to the prom. My teen years were so confusing to me because I didn't feel like I fit in anywhere. I was a very good athlete, so you would think I would have felt included. However, the reality is that I really just put on a brave face. I didn't really know who my real friends were or how I measured up in the eyes of the high school boys because I allowed a comment from a wild six-year-old to cloud my judgment.

Now, even as an adult, I have flashbacks to that little girl when someone says to me, "You are such a catch; how come you aren't married yet?" Well, if I'm such a catch, why have I not met Mr. Right? There are three billion people on this great planet; you can't tell me that not even one man is right for me. Thank goodness we are now exploring Mars; maybe there are more options for finding a man! The longer he hides, the more I start to push Play on that little girl's voice again. I've prided myself on never being a woman who has needed to define herself by her relationships with men. Still, more validation now and again would have been welcome. It's nice to be wanted and courted.

It wasn't until I started writing this book that I realized my issue of fitting in really stems from my relationships with women more than men. As I have peeled back the layers of my onion, I have learned that validation from women has become far more important to me than any attention from men. Years of therapy have helped me to identify my areas of insecurity and to work hard at trying to silence the doubt. To write this book and be anything less than fully authentic would feel like a farce. I don't want you as the reader to feel like this is just one big sob story about broken relationships and lack of self-esteem. In future chapters, I'm going to talk about how I have used these wounds to build the life I want and to create some fabulous experiences. I wanted to share the good, the bad, and the hideous with you because I think it's important that you know the whole story.

I've had women tell me that they admire me; students have said they want be like me when they grow up; and I have been validated for my professional accomplishments through awards. That's all exciting, and I appreciate the kudos, but what's important for you to understand is that nothing is what it seems. If you are a woman who has had setbacks, a broken heart, a dysfunctional childhood, a rough time, or a lack of self-esteem, I'm here to be your champion. There are some things in life we can't control, but what we can control is how we respond to those things.

After years of being depressed, I have chosen to no longer let that be the energy that fuels me. Anyone you aspire to be like has probably had plenty of bumps in the road along the way. It's easy to see only success, but little is ever known about the journey it took for that person to get there. If you take no other message away from this book, please understand that you are just as special as I am, clearly as talented, if not more so, and equally as deserving of a beautifully rich life full of amazing experiences. Find a way to stop competing against yourself; give yourself permission to design the life you want and to start creating the opportunities you seek.

The Bottom Dwellers

I'm about to make a politically incorrect statement: Women aren't always nice to each other, and we can be our own worst enemies! I know that goes against the sisterhood and the notion that we are all in it together, but news flash: we aren't! Worse than a woman not supporting the cause, is a woman who backstabs and undermines the hard work and talent of those who were also born with two X chromosomes. Funnily enough, I'm still to this day surprised when I encounter women who are doing more harm than good. Forget competing for the glass ceiling. If we don't figure out how to authentically support each other, we are never going to get off the elevator on our way to the top.

Several years ago, a friend and business colleague, by the name of Alicia and I were working on several projects. We found opportunities to create synergy whenever it made sense. I had been a founding member of an executive women's group because I liked the mission and intention of the organization. The founder of the organization was a great champion for women, and she wanted to create a space for executive women to gather and learn from and to support each other. Sign me up—I'm all for that. This was great until I found out she really wasn't any of those things, and her personal agenda was really the most important.

As I became more involved with the organization, I could see ways where Alicia and I could partner with the group to create unique programs for the members. Alicia is abundantly talented in the area of sales and business development, and I could bring the event-management expertise to create purpose-driven programs. We invited Sally to lunch one day. Sally knew that Alicia and I were good friends, and she was interested in meeting with her because she had heard about her from several sources. Alicia is, by design, a unique character. She is smart as a whip, has the personality of an entire cast on Broadway, and has a wicked sense of humor. She is the kind of woman that you will never forget once you meet her. She wears bright red lipstick. (I'm more of a pink girl.) She has jet-black hair and loves vintage fashion; I'm blonde and am just praying another girl at the event isn't wearing my dress. If I had a dollar for every time that has happened, I would be rich! I should start to design my own clothes—circa 1991 prom—and would find the entrance into events far less stressful. Alicia and I are complete opposites, but luckily that is what made her ying and my yang work.

We used lunch as an opportunity for Alicia and Sally to get to know each other. Eventually, we broached the subject of partnering among our three companies, and the conversation seemed promising. Sally laughed at our jokes, our natural chemistry, and wanted to know more about the depth of our friendship. When we parted ways, opportunities for synergy seemed optimistic.

A few weeks later, Alicia informed me that Sally had called her and wanted to get together with her to discuss a few projects. We both assumed she was hoping to get Alicia's help with sales and business development. I don't think Alicia even had her seatbelt fastened before she was dialing my phone after their meeting. During their lunch, Sally informed her that she didn't think I was a very good friend because I was trying to keep her (Alicia) all to myself. This made no sense. Sally went on to say that I wasn't marketing Alicia's services, and I was trying to be detrimental to her success. Alicia informed Sally that this was not her experience with me, and instead found that I was very supportive of her and her business. Alicia and I had an unwritten understanding that we wouldn't waste each other's time; if one of us encouraged the other to take a meeting it was because we had vetted the other person and we thought the meeting would be of value. Neither one of us is a big fan of having coffee meetings or lunch dates unless they are going to lead to a new partner, a business opportunity, or a great addition to our circle of influence. We respected each other's time, and we would not make introductions casually. I thought there was value in introducing Alicia to Sally; I didn't realize the idea was going to backfire. Sally was trying to convince Alicia that the two of them should do business together, and she didn't see value in including me.

Let me circle back just so we are all on the same page: Sally is the woman who started an organization to support women—as in help to bring women along, be supportive of the sisterhood, celebrate the contributions women can make when they all work together, blah, blah, blah … I was a founding member of her organization because I believed in the cause. Nothing I was hearing from Alicia about her lunch with Sally supported the mission of the organization that Sally had created. What would motivate Sally to undermine my relationship with Alicia? Her plan completely failed. Not only did Alicia call me immediately to confess what had happened, but we both lost all respect for Sally at that moment, and we decided against moving forward with the projects we had all originally discussed. I refused to further support a woman with questionable ethics, so I terminated my membership with her organization. I guess that situation didn't really go the way she planned, did it?

The great Maya Angelou once said, "The first time someone shows you who they are, believe them." Sally showed her true colors, and I chose to believe who she really was. It would be easy to make excuses, try to justify her behavior, and give her a second, third, or fourth chance, but that wouldn't serve me well. When it comes to doing business, I want to surround myself with people who are ethical, supportive, and help lift me up, not those who want to tear me down. Too often, we don't give ourselves permission to just walk away, and we stay in relationships, both business and personal, that do nothing but bring negative energy into our lives.

Sally and I have many colleagues in common. I've decided to take the much higher road and say nothing to any of them about my concern with her ethics. I think people should cast their own judgments. I voted with my feet and by cancelling my membership in her organization. Alicia was smart enough to see right through

Sally, and she also chose to avoid opportunities to support her work. Some might say that we are not choosing to support the sisterhood if we have cast aside one of the sisters. However, I don't think it serves the cause in any positive capacity if we allow behavior like that to poison the pool.

It would be a challenge to find two women outside of Alicia and me who support the efforts of women more than we do. We are whole-hearted supporters, and we have given our time, energy, and expertise to plenty of women who have asked for our help. Still, I refuse to support any woman or man who has the audacity to try to undermine my business and my integrity, especially with a friend. I'm not going to question myself as I try to justify Sally's behavior; instead, I'm going to continue creating my own opportunities and let my success speak for itself. Don't stand in your own way. Learn from the experience and give yourself permission to move on.

I wish that my experience with Sally was the only time I have encountered a woman who has her personal agenda at stake. But as an experience I had while teaching will show, it's not.

I have had the pleasure of teaching at both the community college level and at the University of San Diego's Event Management Certificate Program for over five years. Teaching will always be one of the greatest opportunities I have ever had. Nothing keeps you on your game, current with your industry, and encourages a continued passion for your craft like teaching the next generation. I am not too humble to say that I am a very good teacher, and I have earned the title of Instructor of the Year by USD. As any of my students will tell you, I am certainly not the easiest professor they will have, but I am very committed to helping them to become successful professionals in their chosen field. It doesn't serve my industry or society at large if I pass the students along because we are just talking about events. Some would think that subject is as easy as underwater basket weaving. I would strongly disagree. I take my chosen obligation as a college professor seriously, and I'm a great champion for the need to educate event planners, so that our entire industry can grow and become even more professionalized.

Therefore, I was stunned when my department chair told me during my evaluation that she had been told that I was bad-mouthing the community college program and encouraging all my students to attend the USD program. I found out that a fellow event colleague we shall call Bonnie told my dean a bona fide lie during an advisory board meeting. Bonnie had expressed her interest in becoming a college-level professor. While she was waiting for an opening, she agreed to be on the advisory board for the department at the college. When my name came up, Bonnie expressed her concerns about having me as a professor in the program. She was "hearing around town" that I was making a mockery of the community college program and trying to get all of my students to just attend the USD program. My department chair told me she was concerned and would have to note that in my personal file. *Nothing* could be further from the truth. I admit that Bonnie and I had a conversation about teaching in both programs, and I would keep my ears open for an opportunity for her to join the faculty. However, at no time did I ever say that I would choose one program over the other.

First of all, the programs focus on different curricula. The community college program is a wonderful overview of the entire hospitality industry with a focus on events, hotels, and culinary management. These students learn both theory and practice and graduate from the program with an associate's degree. The USD program, by contrast, is specialized for event students, and its structure is radically different. In the USD program, students are entrenched in event planning from concept to completion. The USD program is a great next step for the community college students, but it in no way replaces that program. Bonnie felt that if she embellished the truth she might create an opportunity for her to join the faculty because I would be asked to leave. I took umbrage with Bonnie's behavior on multiple levels. Nothing makes me lose my mind faster than someone who is intimidated and therefore uses lies to get ahead. I found myself having to defend my integrity to my department chair because she didn't know who was telling the truth. In the end, I think she realized that Bonnie was indeed not merely embellishing the truth, but creating a fairy tale. With Bonnie and Sally as friends, who needs enemies?

I may forgive, but I never forget. Ironically, several months later, Bonnie contacted me to ask for some advice on how to structure a proposal she was building. You can imagine my scoff when I read her email. Still, instead of completely dismissing her, I answered her questions. I will always try to take the high road. Like with Sally, I am socially pleasant with Bonnie when we run into each other around town, but I make no effort to engage these women who are in the basement.

One of my clients, a professional artist, was recently telling me a story about one of her art students, whom she had to fire. For over ten years, Concetta had taught Jamie how to paint with oils. Concetta is an internationally recognized contemporary impressionist who just recently was diagnosed as a tetrachromat. This means that she has a fourth receptor on her eye, and this allows her to see over 100 million shades of color. The normal eye has three receptors and can discern only one million colors. This recent identification by Dr. Jay Neitz, the leading researcher in this area, has added a significant layer to her already-interesting story. Because Concetta is so talented, it's not unusual for students to want to study with her in private lessons.

Concetta and Jamie had a long history. Over the years, Concetta has served as art instructor, therapist, addiction specialist, and surrogate mother to Jamie. The private lessons were not inexpensive, and over the years, Jamie has paid a significant amount of money to Concetta. As a result, Concetta came to rely on that money as a significant part of her income. It was a hefty sum each month, and all she had to do was help Jamie to become a better painter and to play the role of life coach.

In the last year, Concetta would wake up anxious on the days that she knew she had to meet with Jamie. She couldn't quite reconcile what was happening. Was Concetta depressed? Mad at her husband? Stressed from owning a successful business? Overwhelmed by being a mother to three children? Actually, no. What was causing Concetta so much stress was this one student, who had started to become like a plague. The negative energy that Jamie brought into the salon every week started to wear on Concetta. She didn't know in the beginning that it was happening. Like the barnacles I mentioned earlier, over time Jamie had become stuck to Concetta.

One day in the midst of yet another crisis Jamie was having Concetta had her ah-ha moment. Concetta realized that this troubled woman was the problem. At first, Concetta could never imagine not having the hefty income that Jamie provided. She was caught between personal happiness and financial freedom. But when the salon became more of a crisis center than an art studio, it was the final straw. After discussing with her husband the financial implications of firing Jamie as a student, Concetta decided that no amount of money was worth the stress this relationship was causing. Jamie was parked in Concetta's basement. Concetta had given Jamie way too much control over her energy and mental well-being in exchange for money. She finally gave herself permission to undo the relationship and to ask Jamie to seek another art instructor.

As business owners, we are often faced with the difficult decision of firing clients. Unless you are making money hand over fist, it's hard to choose to reduce your monthly income, but being a slave to clients is not healthy either. Like the personal relationships we allow, as business owners we sometimes allow our clients to be our basement dwellers. How can we grow if our clients are holding us back? It really comes down to giving ourselves permission to make the difficult decision. So often, when one door closes, another opens. However, until we give ourselves permission to hold true to our values, ethics, and entitlement to personal happiness, we can find ourselves competing with clients and the voices in our head.

The Party in the Penthouse

As I look back over my life, I am blessed to be able to name numerous people who are the party seekers in my penthouse! These are my cheerleaders, my yes-you-can crew, and my "I'll help you get anywhere you need to be" gang. These are the people that regardless of what challenge I might be having, they are parked in my penthouse, and they are doing everything they can to help me move from complacence to excellence.

Two years into running my own business, I was talking to a very good family friend named Ian. Along with his beautiful wife Beverley, Ian has created several successful businesses. I enjoy talking with him about being an entrepreneur, and I have relied on his advice regarding several business issues in the past. When I lamented to him one day about the challenge I was experiencing by working at home, he made a generous offer to me. He had recently purchased two brand new buildings for his printing company, and he had excess space. He told me that he and Bev would love for me to share an office with them and their company. I was certainly not seeking a handout from them, but was humbled by the invitation. I thanked him for his generosity but said that I was not in a place to take on a rent obligation at the time. He told me, "Don't be silly. Bev and I want to help you be successful. If inviting you into our office can help you on your journey, that is payment enough." I was stunned. I never want to be a burden to anyone so I had to think long and hard about their offer. I certainly didn't want business to get in the way of our friendship. At the same time, I realized that I was standing in my own way. My fear of being a burden (my words, not his) had me initially thinking I would turn down such an amazing gift. What was I thinking?

Thankfully, I took Bev and Ian up on their generous offer, and I have now shared my office with them for the past four years. The day they put my company name on the front door, I cried. They did not see me as a burden or just a guest. Rather, by putting my name on the door, they have endorsed me and have helped to make me feel like a real business owner. I now have a professional address, a space to meet clients and vendors, and I benefit from the office interactions without having to justify my time, my work, or my absence. Bev and Ian are two of the greatest friends I have ever known, and they remain unbelievably supportive of my journey. They are party people in my penthouse. Creating a business that is successful and makes my heart happy is how they have asked to be repaid. Four years into this arrangement, we are closer as friends than ever. Most of all, I am still humbled by their generosity, and that is important. I never want them to think that I take their gift for granted. They have a stake in my success, and I owe it to them to create an empire I am proud of owning.

You may not have a Bev and Ian in your life that can gift you office space, but I have no doubt if you tell your penthouse party people in your circle what it is that you need, there are plenty of people who can help. Have you ever noticed that when someone asks you "How are you doing?" your response is probably "Fine"? What does *fine* really mean? To me it means complacent. It means content, and it means I'm not growing and stretching. I hate fine. Why don't we ask "How can I help you?" instead of "How are you?"

In one of my professional networking groups, a colleague conducted what she called a *needs ladder* during one of our meetings. We were all asked to tell the group three things that we currently needed in order to help grow our businesses. The rules stated that the need had to be specific. For instance, I might have said, "I'm looking to be introduced to the marketing manager at XYZ Company" instead of saying, "I'm looking for an introduction to small or mid-sized companies in San Diego." The more specific the ask, the more likely someone could help you instantly. If I don't know what you need, how do I know how to help you? What might seem like a challenge to you could be as easy as me making a phone call to a contact, personally introducing you. We are all guilty of spinning our wheels trying to find answers on our own. More than likely, if we'd just open our big mouths and ask our party people in the penthouse for help, we would save ourselves a lot of time and effort. Stop being fine and start telling others what you need! Get out of your own way and give yourself permission to ask!

Someone who has a permanent seat in my penthouse is my dearest friend, Becca. Our families both bought brand-new houses on the same street in 1975. Becca and I were not even two years old yet. Fast-forward to today, and you can count thirty-eight years of friendship. She is like a second sister to me, and we have endured childhood, marriages, deaths, broken hearts, and our greatest joys together as family. Her brother Sean and my sister Jodi are the same age, and so the four of us grew up together on a sleepy little street in San Diego. I was Becca's maid of honor at her wedding, and I was honored when she and her husband Mike allowed me to be in the delivery room for the birth of their third and fourth children. As if being in the delivery room was not a big enough privilege, Becca and Mike asked me to be the godmother of their third daughter, Brooklyn. That will forever be one of the most spectacular days of my life.

On the surface, Becca and I live very different lives. She has a PhD and is a full-time college professor. She has been married for a long time, and is mother to four unbelievable children. I'm an entrepreneur, a really great godmother and bordering on being a spinster—what is the official age that happens? Maybe I should go with cougar!

Over the past thirty-eight years of friendship, there have been endless moments when Becca has been my greatest cheerleader, but nothing has touched me more than something special that happened recently. It's no secret that I am on the verge of turning forty. I was recently at my OB–GYN because of a ruptured cyst. Not that my girly parts are really any of your business, but as I was meeting with the doctor about my test results, his first question to me was, "You're turning forty this year. What are you doing about having a baby?"

I thought, "Um, at the moment my ovaries are very angry with me, and I'm doubled over with pain." The idea of conceiving a miracle wasn't really high on my agenda. I've never been a girl that has longed to be a single mom by choice. For some women, that is desirable, and I have nothing but respect for their choice. It's just not how I ever saw myself becoming a mother. My Cinderella glasses led me to believe that I would find the right man; we would get married, and then I would start spawning adorable humans from my uterus.

My OB–GYN doesn't really care about the fairy tale. Instead, he's looking at my reproductive age and has essentially started the timer for me without my approval. He told me I'm too old to freeze my eggs, so I should either consider a sperm donation immediately or start my online dating profile in hopes of finding an eligible man with strong swimmers. Oh, and if that wasn't enough fun, he said that possibly I would have to have my ovary removed because of the cysts that have decided to take up residence. They did more tests to determine if it is indeed just a cyst or if it is ovarian cancer. Ten minutes with the doctor had turned my spunky smile into tears, and I was suddenly faced with my own reproductive options and the fear that I could lose some of the parts that make me female. That was a mood-boosting appointment.

Becca and I tell each other everything, so it was about thirty seconds after leaving the doctor that I texted her with his advice: Either I get "spermed up" at the bank, or I start scouring eHarmony. He made it clear that my time clock is ticking. I told her that the diagnosis lies somewhere between an ovarian cyst and cancer, and the chance of my getting pregnant at this point is probably very slim. This is her actual text back to me:

> Oh, my sweet friend ... You are so amazing and you will find the right guy. Freezing your eggs is still an option and "we" could always "have" a baby together.

The tears came again when I read her text. What Becca was reminding me of again was her promise that she would be a surrogate should I ever need her. She's a baby machine. I've watched her deliver two of her four babies, and I have never been so impressed and in awe of my friend's strength. Becca is one of those women who can get pregnant just at the simple thought of it! She and her husband quietly discuss it, and it's like her body goes into overdrive. By saying "we" could always "have" a baby; Becca was saying to me that I'm not alone in this journey. She will stand by me, hold my hand, and even carry my baby if need be. That is the most penthouse cheerleader thing she could ever say to me! How unbelievably lucky am I that the two-year-old girl I met as a neighbor would offer to give me the greatest gift decades later? Thank you, Dionne Warwick; that is indeed "what friends are for!" The doctor made me feel like I have very few reproductive options at this point. With one text, Becca proved him wrong.

I understand that not everyone is going to have a friend who is willing to carry her baby for her, but I do hope you have someone in your life that loves you and supports you like Becca and I love and support each other. If anyone in your circle is taking up space in the basement instead of staking claim in your penthouse, it's time you clean house. Do not settle for anyone less than a Becca in your life!

Ask Yourself

Who is taking up valuable space in your life? Are they serving you in a positive or a negative way?

Could you write down the top ten people in your life, outside of family, who either lift you up or keep you down?

Who are your bottom dwellers from the basement, and who are your cheerleaders from the penthouse?

Can you name your personal "Becca?"

CHAPTER FIVE

Permission

Dream and give yourself permission to envision
a you that you choose to be.

—Joy Page

ARE YOU A PERSON WHO WAITS FOR PERMISSION, OR do you ask for forgiveness? By just watching you cross the street, I could probably guess which side of the coin you favor. Once the red hand changes to the white walk man, the signal gives us permission to proceed with caution. If you wait for the light to change, you probably only walk in the crosswalk, too! Have you ever been to New York City or London and tried to wait to cross the street? If so, you would be run over by the crowd behind you walking against the light. Of course, I'm not advocating that you hurl yourself into traffic and play a game of Frogger with the cars on the road. That would be just plain foolish. But why do you stand on the corner waiting for the light to change when there are clearly no cars coming? When you can plainly see that the road is safe to cross, why do you keep standing still? Does the red hand really have that much control over you? What you are really doing is waiting for permission.

I use this analogy as a way to begin a discussion about

permission. It's no accident that the title of this book is *Permission*, because this concept is a driving force behind living the life that is authentically your own. If you are always waiting for the white walk man to tell you to proceed, how much time are you wasting by standing still?

By formal definition, permission is the offering of consent or authorization. We wait to be called on by raising our hands; we wait for the ticket-taker to grant us entry; we seek consent from our parents to stay out past curfew. Our lives are intertwined with permission-worthy moments. Sometimes we give permission, yet in other moments we wait for authorization. What if you decided to stop waiting for permission and instead ask for forgiveness? I'm not authorizing (there's the word!) you to start breaking the law or to lie, steal, and cheat; but we all put way too much stock into receiving permission from others and not enough into granting it to ourselves.

Getting to a point where you can forgive is a power position, but forgiveness is a choice. It's not something we should wait to receive from someone else, but instead should be a quality we grant ourselves. I'm always in awe of people who are able to forgive the monster that has murdered their child or the woman that can forgive her rapist. At some point, the victims of these horrific crimes realize that in order to heal, they have to forgive. They do the work necessary to forgive because they are tired of being in a position of feeling stuck. It's understandable why forgiveness is a virtue that is preached in many religions. It provides a great capacity to love— maybe not the perpetrator, but instead to love yourself enough to move forward.

When you are stuck in a place of not being able to forgive, it feels like you have pulled up to the parking gate, but it won't lift to let you out. You can see life on the other side, but yet you feel frustrated by feeling stuck. You know you have to pay the toll. Granting forgiveness is the toll. Once you do the work and you can reconcile the emotion, the anger, the sadness and the hurt, payment is made, and the gate can lift. As you drive under the gate, permission propels you forward. A lack of forgiveness keeps you stuck, feeling like you are rocking back and forth over the tire spikes and driving the wrong way. Permission, on the other hand, allows you to put your car in gear and drive forward with the flow of traffic and with all four wheels intact.

The energy we expend festering in emotion caused by break-ups, job loss, economic instability, and tragedy keeps us spinning instead of moving forward. Give yourself permission to take the time you need to process the emotion, reconcile the situation, and work toward forgiveness. I realize that this doesn't happen overnight, and time is what heals all wounds. Still, remember that forgiveness is a choice. It's time to give yourself permission to move forward.

With my break-up with Jack and the depth of my broken heart, I was looking for a quick fix to try to get past the pain. But the truth is a funny thing; it will always find you. As long as you keep pretending you are healed or ignoring the "stuff" you need to deal with, you just exist. I certainly was in the months following the night I saw him walk away forever. Funny thing is that given how close we were for so many years, Jack would have been the first person I called when something this major was consuming my life. I couldn't turn to him; he was a contributor. Several months later, I was on a plane to meet my friend Marley in Cabo San Lucas, Mexico. She and I were conducting a workshop there for event professionals and entrepreneurs. As I was on the flight, I took the time to journal everything that still existed in my soul about Jack. I scribbled my disappointment, my love for him, my sadness, the lies I had been told, what was still left unresolved in my heart, and all of the joy he once brought to my life. There was no organized thought to anything I wrote, but I allowed the floodgates of emotion to finally speak. I continued to add to the journal as I spent three amazing days in Cabo. I always love Cabo because the environment for me is conducive to soul-searching and peace. It brings me this serenity through its perfect scenery and culture. Most go to Cabo for the party; I go to reconnect with my heart. Before I would allow myself to get on the plane to come home, I once again read everything on the pages that defined my relationship with Jack. I refused to bring that burden home with me, so as my row was called to board the plane, I walked to the trashcan. Slowly I ripped up all the pages, and then I dropped them in the trash. In that moment, I also asked the universe to shift the hurt and burden I had carried to Jack. I realize, of course, that was not physically possible, but the emotional release and self-talk—telling myself that it was now his turn to reconcile the break-up—were very healing. I could no longer carry the load. It felt like I was living in quicksand. I returned from Cabo feeling emotionally lighter. That's not to say, of course, that I just woke up the next day and asked "Jack who?" But doing the emotional work in Cabo was an important first step toward my healing.

I found that a big part of getting through my break-up with Jack came from forgiving myself rather than forgiving him. I was in Edinburgh, Scotland, for a speaking presentation, and it had been about fifteen months since I had last seen Jack. My parents and I were sitting in a quaint pub in the heart of Edinburgh. The frenetic rain that fell on their umbrellas matched only the scurry of the locals going about their business. The fire roared inside the pub as we enjoyed lunch. For some reason, Jack's name came up in the conversation. I remember my mom asked, "Do you forgive him?" and my response took a moment. Then I said, "I've realized that forgiving myself has been more important than forgiving him." My parents applauded the insight.

You see, I realized that I had been a fool to ever believe in the idea of Jack. As much as I loved and defended him, the reality is that it never matched the authenticity of our friendship. I assumed his same behavior would eventually yield a different result. Isn't that the definition of insanity? Realizing that I had allowed myself to be made a fool over and over again was very hard for me to swallow. In spite of everyone around me, including some of his good friends, telling me the relationship was never going to serve me well, I trusted my love for him. To heal, I couldn't worry about forgiving him. Instead, I put the energy into forgiving myself. I had to reconcile what was happening in my own head that allowed me to be an active participant in a doomed relationship.

Jack continued to show me who he really was; I just chose to not believe him. His behavior was always the truth, not his words. Love blinded that from me for a long time. Jack is certainly far from perfect, but to put all of the blame on him for the demise of our friendship is unfair. It takes two to tango. When you know better, you do better. By forgiving myself, I gave myself permission to start doing better. When I think of him now, I try my best to just bathe him in love and light. I hope he is happy. I hope the blonde is indeed his perfect match and together they have built a great life. Ironically, I can use his same words when I realize that forgiveness "has nothing to do with him."

Permission Is Most Powerful When You Are Living an Authentic Life

What does it mean to give yourself permission? By my own definition, permission is most powerful when you are living an authentic life. Permission is living no longer at the direction of others. Permission is saying what you need to say whether the other person wants to hear it or not. Permission is standing on your own two feet and being completely comfortable in your own skin. Permission is honoring your authentic intention and putting a plan into place to make it happen. Permission is turning self-doubt into self-motivation. By my own definition, permission is action with an understanding of consequences.

I purposely use the word *consequences* because every action has a reaction. If I want to travel around the world for the next year, I need to be able to afford to make that happen. I might grant myself permission to take the trip, but the consequence is that I have to save the money or that I might not have the same job when I return.

I'm not trying to imply that once you give yourself permission, you have an open checkbook and a green light in every aspect of your life. Instead, what I am really referring to is a state of mind and a personal commitment. Harvey MacKay said it best: "A dream is just a dream. A goal is a dream with a plan and a deadline."

The concept of permission started to resonate strongly with me as I traveled around the country presenting my stories and experiences in speaking engagements. As I mentioned in the opening chapter of the book, I kept hearing the word *permission* when women would talk to me after my speech. Whatever I was saying to the audience was hitting home with some of the attendees. When I talk about my struggles, my disastrous relationships, and my battle with depression, some women can relate. On the surface, I can see why some would be impressed with what I have accomplished. By the time I turned thirty-five, I had created an impressive résumé for myself: two-term president for the International Special Events Society—check; earned the Certified Special Events Professional designation granted by ISES, which currently only three hundred people in the world hold—check; a long and distinguished career in corporate America—check; a business owner and entrepreneur—check; created a revenue-generating niche in my industry—check. And the list goes on. I read well on paper. Good for me!

There is a reason magicians use smoke and mirrors in their acts: not all things are what they seem. From the audience's perspective, I have my shit together. Behind the scenes, the shit was often hitting the fan. Haven't you read the first half of this book? Hello, train wreck! Given what I knew to be the real story and not just the one the audience was learning through my PowerPoint presentation, it took me a long time to get comfortable with the word *permission* when the women would come up to me in tears. "Your story has given me permission to make some changes in my life," one woman said. Another—through her tears—told me she has been waiting for a sign, and hearing my story was the permission she needed to start her own business and stop going to a job she hated. What was I saying that was resonating with these women? To me, I was just telling my story and hoping I wouldn't get hammered on the speaker evaluation form. I had to find out what was really going on that was generating this reaction.

As I started to pay closer attention to what the women were really saying, I realized that their stories are really not that different from mine. When I talk about being disappointed that there wasn't traffic on the highway so I could justify being late to the law firm, women tell me they felt exactly the same. When I talk about feeling like a square peg in a round hole in corporate America, women tell me they feel like they don't fit, either. When I tell my story about being broken-hearted and in the wrong relationship, they nod their heads with agreement because they have experienced that situation, too. But where our stories start to diverge is what I did regardless of all the challenges I have faced. I gave myself permission to keep trying to design the life I had imagined. I stopped hoping and started doing.

Without giving myself permission, I would never have left Colin or Jack. Without my own permission, I would never have started my own business. Without my own permission, I would not have spent seven weeks in London working the Olympics in 2012. No one gave me permission to make any of those changes—no one other than me! I've learned that the only way out of the pain and disappointment my delicate little heart has experienced is to create opportunities for myself. I can always count on myself. That devotion to realizing what I want in life, taking action, and persisting by always trying again, has completely changed my business and my life.

I wish the same for you. That is the sole reason I wrote this book—so that you can meet someone who has not led a flawless life yet is working hard to make the life she leads fabulous. I'm no different than you are ... I promise.

If you are working two jobs, are a single mom and barely making ends meet, the last thing you need is some chick preaching to you about giving yourself permission to design the life you want. I get it. Permission doesn't immediately pay your rent, nor does permission feed your kids. If it were that easy, we would all give ourselves permission to win the lottery! I want this book to be a realistic approach for helping you to build a plan, so that you can stop competing against yourself, against society, against your obligations, and against whatever else is hindering you and you can start creating the life you want to live. I honor that you might be struggling, and that life may feel like it is living you a lot more than you are living life. Just finding the strength to take a shower some days is enough of an accomplishment. Until you are really ready in your head, heart, and gut, nothing I can tell you will make a difference. If at the moment you can't find the strength to make any changes, perhaps you should pick up this book again in a month and glance through it when the timing feels right. It's a process, I know.

If, however, you feel like there is a reason you are reading this book at this particular juncture, then I hope you will take inspiration from all these stories, and that they motivate you to take action.

A few years ago, my cousin Tracy dropped a bomb on the family. After nearly twenty years of marriage and three children, she was leaving her husband. I realize this is not a new story; many women find the courage to change their marital status. What is significant to note, though, is that Tracy had limited resources to accomplish the goal. And when I say limited, I mean barely existent. You have more fuzz in your belly button than she had dollars in her account.

Several years before, when I was visiting her in Seattle, she and I had a heart-to-heart talk. I knew she had not been happy for a while, but hearing her admit it was powerful. It felt like she needed to say it out loud for it to really be true. For so long, she had buried her unhappiness. In fact, she had played the role of stay-at-home mom for almost the entire length of her marriage.

Tracy was a stay-at-home mom by choice. She felt her work was to be the constant in the lives of her three children. She thrived on being involved in the PTA, the carpools, and the scrapbook circle with other stay-at-home moms. Let's just call a spade a spade: She really had no desire to work outside the home. She enjoyed her mini-van driving life and the hectic schedule that the life of three busy children brings. Her husband had a sales manager position that required him to travel for weeks out of the month. Tracy became used to being the sole parent for all intents and purposes. On the day she told me she wasn't happy, I secretly thought that she would be all talk and no action. She didn't have the financial resources to leave her husband, nor was she really prepared to go through the process and then support herself after the divorce was final. Although this goal seemed out of reach, I could see the sadness in her eyes as she resigned herself to being stuck. She put the thought of divorce into the "one day after the kids are grown" file in her mind.

What worried me the most about Tracy was that she had allowed herself to get into a position where she didn't have her "fuck-off money." (a commonly used phrase I did not coin.) Although my mother would never use the word *fuck* (and she's cringing at my potty mouth as she reads this), she taught my sister Jodi and me the greatest lesson. Regardless of whether you are married for life or how successful you ever become, you always need to have enough resources saved to make a change. Lack of money should never be the reason you stay in the wrong relationship, in the wrong job, and live in the wrong house. Every woman needs to have her fuck-off money at her disposal. My mom taught us this lesson (in a far more delicate way) at a very early age.

Even being married to my father for nearly forty-six years, where together they have been well employed and financially comfortable, my mom still champions the importance for women to always be able to take care of themselves. Life is hard, and bad things happen. Therefore, she never wanted us to be in a position where we were held hostage to a man or a job if we ever wanted to get out. Money is never the reason you stay. The day Tracy told me she wanted to get out but felt like she couldn't, I realized she didn't have her f-off account.

Shortly after our conversation, Tracy's husband decided to take the severance package his company was offering because he was unhappy with the work he was doing and the travel schedule he was forced to keep. The next two years, while Peter was looking for work, put even more strain on their relationship. Unbeknown to all of us, it was during that time when Tracy found her courage. The architect in her life spoke up and figured out how she was going to get out of a marriage that she no longer wanted to be in.

For the record, the fact that Peter lost his job was certainly not the reason she left him, but it did contribute. Unemployment, depression, and the stress of money issues are never a good recipe for a solid marriage. I believe Tracy had checked out of her marriage many years before the loss of Peter's job. The financial spiral they were in just became the catalyst for making the necessary change. Although she knew it was going to take every ounce of her spirit, every penny she had left, and all the strength she could muster, Tracy finally gave herself permission to end her marriage. I was not surprised she no longer wanted to be married to Peter. I was just very surprised, however, that she had actually put the plan in motion.

Tracy felt that the only option she had financially was to move from Seattle to Phoenix to live with her family. The day she confessed to Peter that she was going to file for divorce and move the children, the atomic bomb went off. Knowing she had to lean on her family for support, she had her sister fly up to Seattle from Phoenix and help take care of the children while their mom and dad had the conversation of all conversations. Imagine the children's surprise when they were picked up from school and instead of going home, they went to a local hotel to see their aunt. Once the plan was put into place, Tracy could only go forward; there was no chance for her to stay stagnant.

For the record, I've always thought Peter was a very nice guy. But being a nice guy doesn't mean he's the right man for Tracy. The bride and groom that stood at the altar twenty years before had evolved into two very different people. Instead of growing together, they ended up growing apart. I have no doubt they both contributed to the demise of the marriage, and to put all the blame on Peter is unfair. Every story has three sides—his, hers, and the truth. He, of course, initially forbade her to leave Seattle with the children. He also refused to move out of the family home, and he froze most of her meager assets. The architect had put the plan in motion. You can never un-ring the bell after that moment.

Without any resources to hire a fancy divorce attorney, Tracy had to dig in and figure out how to single-handedly divorce Peter. Erin Brockovich should play her in the made-for-TV movie. There is a reason it is far easier to get married than to get divorced—I think the courts don't actually want you to do it. The process is impossible, especially when you are trying to teach yourself the law and navigate the legal system. For four months, Tracy was up to her eyeballs with court hearings, motions, endless forms, settlement offers, mediation, and child support decisions. I think she lost twenty pounds, hardly slept, and had to exist in the same house with the man she was divorcing, while balancing the welfare of three great kids. She and I would talk frequently on the phone, and I could hear the exhaustion in her voice. Little by little she made progress. Little by little she figured out how to navigate the court system all by herself. Little by little she managed a move from Seattle to Phoenix to start a new life. Permission and resolve give you strength. Even in her darkest moments, when she would cry more than she would laugh, Tracy figured it out. She found the strength to say fuck-off to the life she had been living and say hello to a life she wanted to design for herself. Applause all around!

After moving to Phoenix, Tracy enrolled in a paralegal program, graduated with honors, reconnected with a great man she went to high school with thanks to Facebook, and started a healthy relationship where she is treated like a queen. Shortly thereafter, she was offered a paralegal position at one of the top law firms in Arizona. All that self-teaching of how to divorce your husband with five dollars to your name had paid off! Had you told her two years earlier where her life was going to end up, she never would have believed the story. I have to admit, I doubted she would actually pull it all off. However, the harder she worked, the more proud I became of her. I'm so delighted she proved my doubt wrong.

It's inspiring to see where she is now in a life she gets to design versus the burden she was carrying for so many years. Both her mind and body are healthier, and she has a spark again in her life that had been dimmed for so long. I have encouraged her to create her own opportunity and start a blog about how to end your marriage without any resources. I know other women would benefit from learning from her story.

Tracy is no different than thousands of women who are in a marriage that no longer serves them. However, what made the difference is her drive and motivation. She stopped talking and actually started doing, and that all came from giving herself permission to do just that. Believe me, if Tracy could pull it off, you certainly can, too. Up till then, she was more involved with bake sales and drama club opening nights at the school. Nothing had prepared her for the fight she was to wage other than the day she finally opened her mouth and let her heart speak. That was the day she remembered that she was in control of the life she wanted to live. Permission granted!

Ask Yourself

Do you wait for permission or ask for forgiveness? Why?

Harvey MacKay said, "A dream is just a dream. A goal is a dream with a plan and a deadline." What deadlines can you put on your dreams?

Who do you need to forgive? Do you need to forgive yourself?

Do you have your "f-off" money? If not, what do you need to do to start saving?

CHAPTER SIX
What Is Your Authentic Intention?

It's never too late to become what you might have been.
—George Eliot

HAVE YOU EVER TAKEN TIME TO HONOR YOUR daydreams? Think about the last time you were on a long run or even driving at a comfortable pace. Where does your mind take you? Is there a thought or idea that resonates more than others? This is really your life's purpose talking to you. I believe we all have an *authentic intention*. In my own definition, an authentic intention is your inner voice; it's whatever is at the top of your "one day I wish I could" list. It's more than just a dream; it's something that is not limited by resources, finances, or access. If you set your mind to it, your authentic intention is always possible. I'm not suggesting you adopt the techniques in *The Secret* and just manifest checks appearing by talking nicely to your mailbox. An authentic intention requires a bit more of an effort than that. Your authentic intention is a thought turned into action by having a plan. The road map begins to appear once you first acknowledge your authentic intention.

You might wonder how you can identify your authentic intention. First, ask yourself when you feel truly energized. If you could wave your magic wand and do anything, what would it be? When is the last time you got lost in an idea or a project?

In my bedroom hangs a motivational quote:

> The Perfect Day
> Going to Bed with a Dream
> Waking up with a Purpose

This exemplifies an authentic intention; which is why when I found this plaque lurking in a small gift shop in Juneau, Alaska, I knew I would find a way to get it packed in my suitcase so it could come home with me. I can wish for no better way to spend a day other than turning a dream of mine into a purpose.

I bet that as you are reading this chapter, your authentic intention is starting to raise its hand, clear its voice, and say, "Hello, I'm in the room!" Please do yourself a favor and start paying attention to what it is saying.

One of my authentic intentions has always been to own my own business. It started speaking loud and clear when I was in college. I was a graduating senior at UC Davis and had finished my course work a quarter early so I had the entire spring quarter to wait before graduation. Instead of just sitting around and watching *Wheel of Fortune* all day, I decided I wanted to have an internship. Back in 1996, the field of event management was still fairly new. For that reason, I wasn't able to pop into the Internship Center on campus and find many opportunities. Never shy about creating my own opportunities, I opened the Sacramento phone book (this was before Google was a verb!) and I started calling party planning companies. I was lucky enough to connect with a woman who owned her own small event management firm. She had previously worked on projects for UC Davis, so she was impressed with the caliber of the students. This gave her enough confidence to invite me for an interview. Katia had never had an intern before, so this was going to be a learning opportunity for both of us.

I passed the interview test, so she invited me to work with her as an intern for twenty hours per week. I would drive my little blue Nissan Sentra across the Yolo Causeway a few days a week, which was particularly brutal without air conditioning. I learned the event management business at her kitchen table. Katia was a single mom, living in a two-bedroom apartment. In the morning, she would fold up her sofa bed, and her bedroom would turn into her office. Although her surroundings were modest, her knowledge and dedication to teaching me the business were robust.

The day after I graduated from UC Davis, I started full time with Katia's company. I went into the internship anticipating that I would graduate with a degree and hang my shingle as a business owner. Remember, I had all that prom coordinating experience, so really what more would I need? What my internship taught me is that I knew nothing about running a business, and it was best to learn my craft on someone else's dime. Although my authentic intention was telling me that I wanted to own a business, I was not close to being ready to make my dream a reality. Just because I knew how to balance my checkbook did not make me a business wizard. There was a lot I still needed to learn.

Once you identify your authentic intention, don't assume that everything in your life will automatically line up. Instead, you should realize that everything you are doing now will eventually lead you to fulfilling your purpose. The journey just becomes more purposeful when you know where you are ultimately headed!

It took me more than ten years from when I set my intention to start my own business until I brought it to fruition. Still, everything I did in those ten years was preparing me for the right timing and opportunity. During this time, while honing my craft as an event manager, I was also exposed to diverse business situations. The day I finally took the leap and left the law firm, I felt far more prepared to hang my shingle than the twenty-two-year-old new grad who thought she knew everything!

Now that you have defined who is in your circle and you have kicked out all of your basement dwellers, the next step toward living your authentic intention is putting it out to the universe. The problem with authentic intentions is that we are often shy about sharing them with others. As mentioned before, "it takes a village," and announcing your authentic intention to your village is key to your success. If I don't know what you need, it's hard for me to help you. The other reason it is important for you to announce your intention is because going public brings with it an important level of accountability. Let me provide an example.

When I first started my business, even long before I left the law firm, I was compelled to announce to the world that I was officially launching my company. It's one thing to tell my parents and those in my close circle about my dream of starting a business. My family, although my biggest cheerleaders, were not going to be my only clients. I knew that in order to grow my business, I needed to make sure that I cast a wide net for publicizing my intention.

One night, while sitting at my little white hand-me-down desk in my tiny one-bedroom apartment, I started writing an email. This was my coming-out email. Without hesitation or fear, I felt it was finally time to tell the world that I was starting a business. My email explained that The Henley Company is an event, travel, and lifestyle concierge firm. I knew when I founded the business that I wanted to continue with my event-production services, but I also had a whole battery of services that I loved to do as well: travel coordination, personal shopping, errand running, household management, and others. Through my own research, I discovered the personal concierge and lifestyle management industry, and I knew that I had found the other side of my business. My company is named The Henley Company because I had the good fortune back in 2000 of living in a town outside of London called Reading. One of the neighboring towns to Reading is Henley-on-Thames, most famous for the Henley Regatta each year on the Thames River. For me, Henley holds more than just notoriety for rowboats. It quickly became my happy place—both personally and professionally. My time in England was glorious, not only from an international business opportunity, but also from an opportunity to cut the apron strings and grow up. Henley is an adorably quaint English town that I instantly fell in love with when I would spend time there on weekends. I made a promise to myself that one day I would name my first child or company Henley. We now know which has come first!

As I finished crafting the email, I began to wonder if I was really ready to make such a big announcement. I moved my mouse to the Send button, and something greater than I told me to pause. I lifted my hand from the mouse and asked myself if the timing was right and if I was ready to no longer hide behind a dream. I knew that once I hit Send, I was inviting the world into my dream. By putting it out there, I was now welcoming accountability. I mean, who wants to be the girl that makes some big announcement and then has to tell everyone she really hasn't done anything to make that dream a reality? Sure enough, when I would run into friends and colleagues, they would always ask, "How is your business coming along?" By sharing my intention, I was creating an invisible advisory board for my business. The people who cared about my success became emotional stakeholders. Feeling obligated to make them proud became the fuel I needed to work every night on The Henley Company. Unless you fully commit to making your business or intention a success and you work long hours and give lots of energy to the project, you are only going to be living a hobby.

If you ever need inspiration by a guy who can move mountains and can turn opportunity into living the dream, look no further than Gary Vaynerchuck of The Wine Library. Do yourself a favor and watch some of his YouTube videos. I purposefully use his videos each semester in my class because he has an unbelievable way to boil life down to the simple and obvious: Do what you love and work really hard. That's the secret. Do what you love and the money and peace will come.

My attempt to start doing what I love came when I finally pushed Send on the introduction to The Henley Company email. And then I started working really hard! Life certainly doesn't get infinitely easier once you identify your authentic intention, but it does provide a road map to your destination, and it creates purpose.

When I was working at the law firm, my office was situated so I could look over the sea of cubicles. Rita, a middle-aged woman with long salt-and-pepper gray hair, sat just outside my door. Every day she would put a Post-it note on her computer monitor that would say "at lunch." I guess it would be appreciated if she were really at lunch so her attorney-bosses knew her status. However, she was often just sitting at her desk, eating her leftover dinner from the night before in Tupperware, and playing solitaire on her computer. The "at lunch" note was a way to say "I'm invisible." She would also leave a note on her computer screen if she was "at the copier" or "in the mail room."

Rita essentially had no autonomy, nor did she care about herself enough to leave her desk during lunch and at least get some fresh air outside the building. It's easy to judge and wonder why she hid behind a Post-it note, but my gut tells me she didn't know any better.

Rita made me sad. She was in her early fifties, never had been married, and had decided that her life was destined for cubicle alley. I'm not saying that she had to have the same ambition as I did to run my own business, which ultimately allowed me to leave the firm. Nor am I suggesting that she needed to claw her way to the corner office and bust through the glass ceiling. Instead, what made me sad is that she never had given herself permission to honor her authentic intention. If you had asked the ten-year-old version of Rita what she wanted to be when she grew up, I doubt that she would have said a law firm secretary, with a Post-it note stuck to my forehead so no one would bother me while I was taking my thirty-minute lunch break. Again, the point here is not that she is a law firm secretary. That takes a certain talent and skill, and Rita excelled in both. What I'm talking about is the sadness in her eyes that represented her concession that her life was only as good as it was, versus a life full of everything it could be.

Through my window, I would watch Rita work. There was hardly life or spirit in her unless she was talking about riding her motorcycle on the weekend, or maybe taking a few days off a year to drive to Las Vegas. I always wondered if Rita had just given up. Was this all she was willing to give to her life? How come she hadn't allowed her authentic intention to speak as loudly as mine was doing? Why had going through the motions become her norm?

To become something different than you already are is not only scary, but it also takes a lot of energy and effort. Rita probably found comfort in the regular paycheck every two weeks and the good benefits the firm offered. I believe we all have a currency we are willing to spend—for some it is the thrill of being an entrepreneur and going against the grain; others like to be cautious and feel safe. There are costs and benefits in both situations. Rita probably fell in the latter category. However, that didn't mean that on nights and weekends she couldn't start designing the life she wanted to really live. I honestly don't think she knew how, and that can be as paralyzing as the fear of succeeding. Her "at lunch" note was more of an analogy for her life. Being invisible to others is one thing; being invisible to yourself is quite another.

I look back at my time working with Rita, and I am sorry that I never made the effort to ask her what her authentic intention in life had been when she was younger or might be now. Perhaps I could have helped her on her journey. Rita sticks with me to this day because she reminds me that I need not remain silent and just a voyeur when I see someone being stuck. Instead, I should take the time to understand people beyond just their obligatory "I'm fine" answer to the standard "how are you" question.

An exercise I have incorporated into my presentations is one centered on the concept of authentic intentions. I share my own example of announcing The Henley Company by email, and the anxiety that came from no longer just talking about my dream, but finally making it a reality. I ask the attendees to write their authentic intentions on an index card I provide. I only give them two minutes to complete the task because I want them to acknowledge the first thought that comes to their minds. This, I believe, is their pressing authentic intention and their real purpose. I always feel the energy change in the room when I start collecting all of the index cards after the two-minute exercise. I don't tell them in the beginning that I am going to collect the cards because it would skew the authenticity of their responses. I explain that I am going to read out each of the intentions to the room because I believe that the universe has to know what it is that you are seeking in order for it and others to help you succeed. I never ask for their names because I don't want them to feel singled out. Some attendees are too shy or feel too embarrassed to tell anyone what their heart wants. For that reason, I take it upon myself to be their Send button. Once I pushed Send on the email I wrote about my company, there was no going back. By reading aloud their authentic intentions, I feel like I am helping them to take the first step toward making their intentions a reality.

I now have a box of hundreds of index cards I have collected from my presentations. It is always a joy to read through them from the front of the stage. Here is just a sampling of the authentic intentions I have helped set free:

» I want to open a bed-and-breakfast in Tuscany.

» I want to travel to the birthplace of my mother and stop hurting from my childhood.

» I want to become financially comfortable so that I can have more fun and less stress in my life.

» I want to lose 100 pounds.

» I want to learn how to speak Spanish fluently.

» My authentic intention is to be a singer and have the courage to appear on stage in front of a live audience.

» I want to create a program for abused children so they know they are loved.

» I really want to go to law school and focus on victims' rights.

» I wish I could repair the relationship with my father.

» I want to open a restaurant that honors the recipes of the meals my grandmother taught me how to cook.

» I want to be able to finish college.

The authentic intentions that I have the pleasure of reading always vary. Sometimes they are career-focused, and others stem from an emotional core. There is no right or wrong answer to be written on the index card, but rather the exercise itself helps to identify their true wish or life's purpose.

I wish that on Rita's infamous Post-it note, she would have written, "My authentic intention is …" instead of "at lunch." Writing it down and sharing it with the world is crucial to making the dream a reality. It's a privilege to help set free the authentic intentions of my audience. There is no going back after their intention is shared—they start to treat their dream differently.

Get Involved

Right now, at this very moment, find an index card and write down your authentic intention. Simply honor the first thing that pops into your mind that speaks to your true passion and life's ambition. I want you to read the index card out loud and then put it in a place you can see every day.

Next, I want you to jump on your email program and send your authentic intention to me. If you aren't ready to send an email out to your sphere announcing your authentic intention, at least send it to me. The act of knowing that someone else knows what you really want, and what will make your heart sing, is an important first step. I promise I will hold your authentic intention with deep respect and encouragement. I pledge that within a few months after you send me the email with your authentic intention, I will contact you for a status report. I promise that knowing you are accountable will make a difference. You won't know when the email, or phone call, or note in the mail is going to arrive from me, but one day it will come. Do you want to admit that you have made no effort toward designing the life you want to live? I won't crack the whip or scold you; how you manage your life is up to you. However, I would bet my last dollar if you knew someone was going to look in on you and hold you accountable for your actions, you would make far more effort than you would in your dreaming phase. Ultimately, my goal is to create a space, either through a blog or on a website, where people can write their authentic intentions (either anonymously or shouting their name out loud) and create a supportive community where we can help each other to accomplish our goals.

I wish you the perfect day. Go to bed tonight with a dream but wake up tomorrow with a purpose.

Email your authentic intention to me at hello@thehenley company.com.

Ask Yourself

What is your authentic intention?

If you are having a problem identifying your authentic intention, ask your friends, family, or co-workers when they see you being blissful. What are you doing? What do you regularly talk about?

If you went to bed with a dream and woke up with a purpose, what would it be?

Are there areas of your life where you are "at lunch?"

What is it that you really want to do and would be willing to work really hard to make happen?

CHAPTER SEVEN
Impossible Versus I'm Possible

Nothing is impossible; in fact the word itself says "I'm possible!"
—Audrey Hepburn

WHEN YOU LOOK AT THE WORD *IMPOSSIBLE,* WHAT do you see? From this point forward, I hope you see "I'm possible." The glorious Audrey Hepburn once said, "Nothing is impossible; in fact the word itself says, 'I'm possible.'" What a beautiful way to turn the negative into a positive.

Positive and negative thoughts can become self-fulfilling prophecies. When I was learning to ski as a child, I remember the instructor saying to me, "You go where you look." If you focus on where you don't want to ski, your mind sends you to that spot. If you don't want to ski into the ditch, don't look at the ditch. Instead of focusing downhill, we become more focused on the obstacles in our way.

We run our lives the same way. As we focus on the impossible and the obstacles we face, it is difficult to see the "I'm possible" in the situation. Instead of focusing on where we do not want to be, we should extend our focus toward where we want to be. The ski instructor always reminded me to look further downhill than always right in front of me. This allowed my mind to make a plan toward what was approaching versus just reacting to the immediate danger.

In my youth, I was a strong skier. My mom reminds me that as a child I used to fall on purpose just to make the advanced runs much more exciting. I had no fear. That is, of course, until I started overthinking everything and I let my fear (impossible) get in the way of my ability (I'm possible). Going to college at UC Davis, I was close to Lake Tahoe and all of its perfect skiing conditions. Every year, my dad, uncle, and friends would come up for a ski weekend. We would head up the mountain to enjoy a few days of powder. Having grown up on the slopes, I had no fear of the challenges the mountains would throw at me.

One day, we all decided to take on the black diamond run at Kirkwood Mountain Resort. The weather was perfect and the sun was shining. We took the long chairlift ride to the top. I had previously skied black diamond runs, but really considered myself more of a solid advanced skier, which is one or two steps below the black-diamond level. With prodding from the group, I agreed to take on the challenge.

At the top of the mountain, the weather conditions were quite different. The wind was blowing at such a force that the snow was pelting us as we glided off the chairlift. The sun was shining late in the day, so shadows were starting to cover the mountain. As we all stood at the top and surveyed the mountain, it was obvious that the biggest challenge was the first fifty yards in front of us. If we could just get through the sheer, steep fifty yards that met us at the top, we would return to skiing essentially a blue intermediate run. This was not the time to think; it was a time to attack.

One by one, our group started down the hill. My uncle and his girlfriend headed straight down. My dad could sense my hesitation; so he started down to carve out our path. My friend Dan and I stood at the top of the mountain and pondered our approach.

In the great family movie *We Bought a Zoo*, the character Benjamin Mee, played by Matt Damon, attempts to foster a sense of courage in his children: "All you need is twenty seconds of insane courage, and I promise you something great will come of it." I could have used this reminder because instead of mustering up the twenty seconds of courage I would need to get past the steep fifty yards of the mountain, I let my head get in the way. With much trepidation, I started down the mountain and slowly Dan followed behind me. Instead of attacking the mountain, I let the mountain take control. As the shadows covered the snow, the snow turned to ice. Anyone who has ever skied knows that hitting a patch of ice can be disastrous. As soon as my skies hit the ice, I crumbled. I gave into the mountain and focused only on the ice, not skiing down the mountain as I was taught. My dad realized that I was in trouble, so he stopped and tried to coach me. The harder I fought the mountain, the more I gave fear control of the situation. I lost my footing and slid about twenty-five feet straight down. I was in an impossible mindset rather than "I'm possible."

My fear took over all rational thought. Faintly, I could hear my dad's words of encouragement, and his lessons on how to flip my skies around so I was headed downhill. I was facing the cliff; it was all I could focus on. Remember, you go where you look. My paralysis from fear had taken over all rational thought, my ability, and my courage. I had done a kick turn with my skis lots of times. Years of skiing had taught me how to get out of this situation, but for some reason on that day, in those conditions, I literally hit the ice and slipped. Rational thought had gone out the window. Keeping my eye on the goal of getting to the bottom of the run left me feeling blind. I was stuck on the impossible mountain.

The more afraid I became, the more I impacted my friend Dan's ability to ski. He was kind enough to stay with me during my episode. However, being a less experienced skier, he took his lead from me. For a while, as I sat in the snow, my only lifeline was Dan's ski pole. He held it out for me so I would feel like I had something to anchor myself to. Like a ski pole was going to really stop me if I started to fall! More than likely, I would have taken Dan with me! No good deed goes unpunished, but I appreciated the effort Dan made. My dad had to sidestep back up the mountain until he stood next to me. Like teaching a toddler to walk, he had to tell me how to move my legs and where to put my skis. Every ice patch felt like a death march for me. I was convinced I was going to tumble hard and really hurt myself. Exhaustion was starting to set in, and I was physically and mentally drained. It took me over two hours to get to a place on the mountain where I felt like I was once again in control. Had I just taken Benjamin Mee's advice and given the situation twenty seconds of courage, I would have already been in the lodge drinking beer.

Sadly, my skiing career has come to an end. The next year, when my family came up for the ski weekend, I was far too tentative, and I again found myself over my head. This time the ski patrol had to bring me down the mountain, and they reprimanded my dad for putting me in a situation that was above my ability. It's not at all his fault; he knew the only way to get me comfortable again with the mountain was to get back on it.

I had allowed myself to become a liability on skis. I was spooked. I've skied a few times since my college days, but I certainly don't attack the mountain like I once did. I was once an "I'm possible" skier. Now, I'm a has-been "impossible" skier who let the mountain and fear win.

Imagine what a difference it would make to us either professionally or personally if we just adopted the twenty seconds of courage mentality. Do you hesitate picking up the phone and making a sales call because of self-doubt? Do you miss the opportunity to introduce yourself to the attractive guy across the room because you are afraid? What if for the next month you committed to using twenty seconds of courage to live boldly? I challenge you to do just that. I want to hear your success stories, so be sure to connect with me via Twitter at @henleyco with hashtag #permission, or email me at hello@ thehenleycompany.com.

I'm drawn to successful business folks. I love to talk business and read my *Entrepreneur Magazine* so I can absorb every ounce of their knowledge and talent. To me, there is no greater entrepreneur than Richard Branson, founder and chairman of Virgin Group. He epitomizes the brilliant business mogul who wants not only to create dynamic companies, but also to play hard in life. He is not driven by money, but rather by developing companies and talented people who do business differently. There is much to learn from an entrepreneur who looks at life through a very different lens.

In the special events industry, I have found it difficult to find truly business-minded folks. One of the curses of the industry is that we are all too creative. We just assume that if we design pretty events, clients will call us. That is far from the truth. If you don't know how to sell your services, you are really just running a hobby.

About a decade ago, I started hearing about a trailblazer in our industry by the name of Marley Majcher. Marley owns The Party Goddess, a high-profile event company out of Los Angeles. She counts Brittney Spears, Snoop Dog, Sofia Vergara, Pierce Brosnan, and Katherine Heigl as clients. When I first heard Marley speak at an industry conference, she was teaching event planners how to make money in their businesses. Believe me when I tell you, *no one* was talking about this at our educational seminars. I was grateful that someone was taking the lead on this topic, even though it was still going to be a few years before I started my business.

I would follow Marley through her webinars, teleseminars, and at industry events. I was a big fan of who she was, the company she had created, and her mission to teach others how to make money. Marley would be the first to tell you that she hasn't always understood how to run a business. This makes her story much more authentic, and she had to teach herself how to make money. Until Marley, no one in the event industry was willing to share the information. Marley set out to learn best business practices. The more she was willing to share the information, the more of a following she created. She didn't set out to be the expert in running a successful event business, but she has become the Pied Piper for the industry.

In 2010, Marley and I were both in New Orleans attending The Special Event Conference and Tradeshow. Marley was one of the speakers, and I made a point of attending her session. I was always inspired by her message and business practices. I arrived a few minutes after the program started, and I found myself in the very last row of a ballroom with three hundred other events professionals. I was taking copious notes as Marley was talking about how event planners frequently leave money on the table. My personal architect decided it was time to engage my twenty seconds of courage.

With three hundred people sitting between Marley and me, I raised my hand. The next thing I heard was "lady in the red scarf in the back row." My business idol had called on me, and this was my chance to engage with her. I commented that although I agreed with everything she was saying about leaving money on the table, one additional way event planners could increase revenue was through self-producing their events. By this time, in my own business, I had taken an original concept and self-produced a revenue-generating event. My first self-produced event was a high-profile, sold-out movie premier for *Sex and the City: The Movie*. Through a strategic partnership, I had created an event that generated significant media interest, sold more than five hundred tickets, and had become my own highest-paying client. I'll talk more about how that process works in a later chapter. However, the "twenty seconds of courage" and the "I'm possible" messages, gave me the backbone to prove to Marley that I was serious about business.

Marley asked me some follow-up questions about the event so that she could fully understand the opportunity for revenue. Then she said to the room of more than three hundred people, "I know you have all come to hear me speak today, but you need to listen to what this woman is telling you." In that moment, three hundred heads turned and looked at me. By raising my hand and finding the courage to contribute to what the expert was already saying, I was able to connect with someone I held in very high esteem. Had I remained quiet and said nothing to Marley that day, I doubt we would have the relationship we have now.

Before I could even get out of my chair after the session, I was bombarded by event planners wanting to know more about my self-producing of events. Marley's endorsement upped my credibility in the industry. Marley encouraged me to come see her after the session was over. I did, and we exchanged business cards. With Marley in Los Angeles and me based in San Diego, we are in relatively close proximity to each other. Several weeks later, Marley and I met for coffee, and I was able to further explain my concept for self-producing events to her. It was a few months before *Sex and the City 2* was coming out in the theatres, and I asked if she would be interested in co-producing the event with me in the LA market. She agreed, and a strategic partnership was forged.

As much as I value the opportunity to do business with Marley, the greatest gift that came from my twenty seconds of courage back in New Orleans is a deep friendship. I adore Marley, not just because she has made herself wickedly successful, but because she is one of the funniest, most genuine, crazy, and authentic people I have ever had the pleasure of knowing. She's firmly cemented in my small but mighty group of women who complete my circle. What started out as a business relationship has yielded a beautiful friendship. She is one of my penthouse party people, for sure! When I was in my darkest moments following the Jack debacle, she told me to block out a day on my calendar. She took the same day off and drove down to San Diego for a day of recess with me. We painted ceramics at a ceramics café in a room full of kids, and we talked until I cried. She knew I was so broken, and she took the time to help me put the pieces back together. She promised not to leave San Diego that day until I had a plan on how to move forward. I had cried enough, and I now knew I was not alone in this journey.

In recent months, I have been able to offer that same level of support to her. I now can recognize that different tone in her voice when she says, "Please come up for the weekend and don't say no." There is a difference between knowing when your friend wants to see you for a play date and when she emotionally needs you. I arrive as her knight in shining armor, and together we slay the dragons. Some days she wears the armor; some days it's my turn. Whatever the situation, we always are able to pick up where we left off and make light of the crazy lives we lead!

From this day forward, please make a commitment that every time you see the word *impossible* you will always remind yourself "I'm possible." Always keep your view well beyond the current ice patch and far down the mountain so you know where you are headed. And most importantly, embrace those important twenty seconds that can literally change your life or your business. I'm confident that if you made these small changes, you will start to see a big difference. Give yourself permission to believe "I'm possible!"

Ask Yourself

What feels impossible?

What is your "I'm possible?"

What could you change if you mustered up twenty seconds of courage?

What are you staring at in front of you that is diverting you from looking downhill? Remember, you go where you look!

CHAPTER EIGHT
All You Need Is Love

Love, love, love. Love, love, love. Love, love …
There's nothing you can do that can't be done.
Nothing you can sing that can't be sung.
Nothing you can say but you can learn how to play the game.
—*All You Need Is Love,* The Beatles

I JUST TURNED FORTY, AND I AM NEARLY SEVEN years into running a business. My thirties were emotional, challenging, the best for opportunity, and full of ebbs and flows. I've experienced the best of the best and the worst of the worst. I learned more in my thirties than in any other decade before. Who I am now is very different than who I was at twenty-nine or nineteen. That's a good thing. If I were to summarize this decade, its overwhelming theme would be "all you need is love." This has been my biggest lesson since crossing the threshold from my third decade.

I'm certainly not saying that all you need is the love of a great man or woman and all your problems slip away. If you have found that kind of love, good for you. My definition of love is much more self-serving. It's entirely focused on doing what makes your own heart sing and living an authentic life.

In Love with Your Business

In earlier chapters, I talked about my decision to leave corporate America to pursue my own business. This was my attempt at falling back in love with my life's work. I had not only fallen out of love with my job when I was with the law firm, but I also felt hopeless about finding anything better. Who wouldn't want to work for one of the best law firms in the country and to have the level of responsibility I was given? There is no doubt that I had a tremendous job. Even though it was not the job I ultimately wanted to keep, I am profoundly grateful for the opportunities I was given while at the firm. I recognize that just because I didn't fit in doesn't mean there is something wrong with corporate America. Part of being in love with your business or career is identifying what it is you really want to be doing.

If you have never taken the time to watch Steve Jobs's commencement address to Stanford University graduates in 2005, please put down this book and do that now. I show the video every semester in my college-level classes. It's chock-full of great life lessons and nuggets to help you design the life you really want to live. Steve Jobs did not live a charmed life. He had his struggles, felt like his path at times was traversing back and forth rather than forward, and he had his share of pain. But somehow, in spite of all the things that would be easy to point out as challenges, Jobs was able to create one of the most successful companies in history. And then he got fired from that same company. Ironic? You bet!

In his commencement address, Steve Jobs said:

> When I was seventeen, I read a quote that went something like: "If you live each day as if it was your last, someday you'll most certainly be right. It made an impression on me, and since then, for the past thirty-three years, I have looked in the mirror every morning and asked myself: "If today were the last

day of my life, would I want to do what I am about to do today?" And whenever the answer has been no for too many days in a row, I know I need to change something.

Remembering that I'll be dead soon is the most important tool I've ever encountered to help me make the big choices in life. Because almost everything—all external expectations, all pride, all fear of embarrassment or failure—these things just fall away in the face of death, leaving only what is truly important. Remembering that you are going to die is the best way I know to avoid the trap of thinking you have something to lose. You are already naked. There is no reason not to follow your heart.

Steve Jobs, Commencement Address,
Stanford University, 2005.

If you are currently going to a job that does not allow you to follow your heart, give yourself permission to stop doing that. I understand you have bills to pay, mouths to feed (either two- or four-legged) and you can't just snap your fingers and create this magical life. However, if you give yourself permission to start designing the life you want to live, it's amazing how you start to follow your heart. We spend approximately one-third of our life at work. Do you want to be spending that time at the mercy of someone else or within your own control?

Again, I understand that being an entrepreneur is not for everyone, so please don't think I'm trying to champion business ownership for all. Instead, what I am trying to convey is that your work should be a vocation, not a chore. Even if you work for someone else, it is highly possible for you to find a position that allows you to thrive.

My dad spent almost thirty years working in higher education, first as a college professor, and then as a dean at a community college, before he retired in 2011. My dad would be the first to tell you that he never worked a day in his life. That's not to say that he didn't encounter challenges, campus politics, or bureaucracy that could be frustrating. Still, he knew every day when he entered the classroom that he was exactly where he was supposed to be.

My mom has spent thirty-six years working for Kaiser Permanente. Over the course of her career, she has held several administrative positions within the organization. Now that my dad has retired, she often gets asked when she will follow in his footsteps. Her answer is always the same: "I'm not ready." Waking up every day, knowing she has a purpose, and going to a job she enjoys is very important to her. She will retire when she feels ready. In the meantime, she is in love with her business, even though someone else is signing her paycheck each month.

These words from Steve Jobs are a great reminder that we should always be in love with our business or vocation. Continuing in his commencement address, Jobs says:

> I'm convinced that the only thing that kept me going was that I loved what I did. You've got to find what you love. And that is as true for your work as it is for your lovers. Your work is going to fill a large part of your life, and the only way to be truly satisfied is to do what you believe is great work. And the only way to do great work is to love what you do. If you haven't found it yet, keep looking. Don't settle. As with all matters of the heart, you'll know when you find it.

A habit I'm trying to break is my addiction to Diet Coke. I love everything about drinking it: the delightful experience that the ice, the straw, and the soda offer. The experience is even better when it comes from a drive-through window. Call me crazy, but I look forward to my late-morning stop at a fast-food restaurant (I know which serve Coke versus Pepsi products!) and placing the order through the drive-through speaker. I love the bubbles and the first sip. Recently, I decided that Diet Coke and I should probably have a break after it told me it was having a baby with someone else. Ha! In all seriousness, I've tried to fall in love with soda water. To my delight, many fast-food restaurants also serve soda water, so I can have the same drive-through experience without the unknown negatives that some say soda can bring. I feel like I'm cheating on Diet Coke when I just order its clear cousin. Still, I'm sure my body appreciates the switch.

As interesting as I am sure you find my daily soda habit, there is a relevance to this story. Recently I stopped at a local Jack in the Box restaurant for my daily vice. The voice that came through the speaker was exceptionally friendly. The woman told me to pull forward and that she looked forward to seeing me. When I pulled up to the window, I had my money prepared. After this many years of the same routine, I knew my habit was going to cost me $2.26. Marta was the voice through the speaker. Before she asked me for my money or handed me my drink, she asked me how my day was going. We exchanged pleasantries, but before I drove away, Marta asked me how was the service I had received. When I told her that I found her to be very friendly, she said thank you and then went on to say, "It's important that you feel welcome here. I've worked at this Jack in the Box for over twenty years," she continued, "and I consider this restaurant to be an extension of my home. I'm delighted you were satisfied with our service because anything less than extraordinary would make me feel like a bad host." I told her that I thought she was fabulous at her job and to keep up the good work.

What a delight to know that this Jack in the Box, so convenient to my office, also served soda water. I was now going to look forward to my daily interaction with Marta. Some might say that working at a fast-food restaurant for twenty years doesn't amount to much, but

I think Marta has found her true calling. Who wouldn't want to be served by a friendly voice, a happy face, and a kind friend through the drive-through window? Marta is more to Jack in the Box than someone who just asks, "Would you like fries with that?" Marta is an ambassador, and she is clearly someone that is in love with her business. I have no doubt Marta knows how the regular customers like their burgers and whether or not they prefer ice in their drinks.

Being in love with your business doesn't mean you have to own a company or hold a C-level position at the firm. Being in love with your business stems from figuring out what you love to do and then doing that—every day! If you are in retail, a mechanic, a postal worker, or a nurse, be the best at the vocation you have chosen. You do yourself a disservice if you settle for anything less than being the Marta in your company. Every position in a company makes a contribution; are you willing to just settle for "at lunch" like Rita at the law firm had done?

If you can't figure out the direction your professional life should be taking, start seeking help. Call someone like Mindy Bortness at Communication Works, Inc. in San Diego and have her conduct personality and communication style assessments. Work with a life coach who can help you to identify where your passion currently exists. Or identify an accountability partner, perhaps either a friend or a colleague, who will hold you accountable for making strides on your professional journey. I'm happy to be that person if you need a pal.

What if you were to start a concierge circle and you met with three to five other women who are looking to make a career transition or to start a business? The group would offer accountability, and together all of you could support each other's efforts.

In the last few years, book clubs have become popular. If your book club has been anything like mine, after we read *Fifty Shades of Grey*, we have spent every other gathering just drinking wine and never once discussing the next book. What was there left to say after we devoured *Fifty Shades*? Imagine if you could take that same time commitment and turn it into a concierge circle, where women could support each other with résumé writing, mock interviewing, wardrobe styling, and creating a plan toward living the life they want to live.

And the more wine the better, I say; I have plenty of good ideas with a glass of Chardonnay! Creating the life or job you want to live doesn't have to be a singular activity. Why not make it a community affair and let the village help you get there? There are a lot of tools available. However, first you have to give yourself permission to truly be in love with your business—whatever your calling happens to be. Before you can fall in love with your business, you need to be in love with you. Knowing what your strengths are and what makes your heart sing are the first steps.

I spend a lot of time in this book talking about careers. Still, I recognize that not everyone aspires to be an entrepreneur or to crawl up the career ladder. My personal definition of feminism states that all women have a choice, and that choice can translate not only in their personal lives but in their professional endeavors as well. If you want to stay at home and raise children, that is a choice you are entitled to make. However, I don't believe women can have it all at the same time. We try our best, but the reality is that there just isn't enough time and energy to go around.

I recognize that if I should ever become a mother, my career will evolve into something different. I don't see myself ever giving up my company completely, but I recognize that to set expectations that I am going to give 100 percent to my work, my future husband, and our offspring is unrealistic. There just aren't enough hours in a day to be all things to all people. While all this recent talk of female executives scolding women for not speaking up at the table or otherwise asserting themselves might sell lots of books, I don't feel the message helps women feel balanced.

I am career-driven, but I'm also still single at the age of forty. I have a lot to be proud of when it comes to my professional accomplishments, but awards and new client contracts don't keep my bed warm at night. I admit it would be nice to have a partner to share my success and challenges with, but that has not been my reality up to today. I attribute a big part of that to not only my shyness with men (see the first part of this book!), but also my dedication to my career. When others my age were out being social, I was probably at my desk trying to launch and grow a business. I'm not complaining and feeling left out. I had plenty of opportunities to partake in social activities; I just chose to focus on work.

I know for a fact that my relationship with Colin would not have survived had I been officially full-time in my business when we were still together. He expected that we would have dinner together each night, and we would enjoy free time together on weekends. It's a completely acceptable expectation for anyone who is not starting a business. We had enough problems as it was. My sudden need to be glued to my laptop for twenty hours a day was certainly not going to help our cause. Colin has every right to assume his girlfriend is actually going to spend a substantial amount of couple time with him each week. I would never have been a good girlfriend living under that assumption for the first three years of running my business. There is no way I could have balanced and been successful at both. Does that make me a bad girlfriend and a good business owner or vice versa? The Henley Company became my boyfriend, best friend, worst enemy, and comfort zone. Even though it was a contributing factor to the demise of my relationship with the man that was keeping me warm at night, it was the choice I made at the time. For me, at that moment, being in love with my business became more important than being in love with a man. Will that always be the case for me? I can't say. But to believe that I could have everything in that chapter of my life was a fairy tale I wasn't willing to pretend existed.

Every woman doing the best she can with the opportunities available to her supports my definition of feminism. If you want to be a stay-at-home mom, great; be completely in love with doing that. If you eventually want to go back in to the workforce, then you must realize that your rusty skills and lack of experience may be a consequence of that choice. My cousin Tracy learned quickly that taking a hiatus from professional work outside the home for twenty years did not set her up for success when she was trying to support herself post-divorce. Staying at home cost her professional skills. It was a choice she made.

I'm not saying you shouldn't make the choice to stay home, but to be anything but realistic doesn't serve us well. To be forty and without a husband (even a starter-husband), has really been my choice. It's easy to complain about not finding the perfect mate and playing the woe-is-me card, but at the end of the day, I'm in charge of how I live my life. For now, I have chosen to be in love with my business.

Unlike me, if you choose to work inside the home, know you have fallen in love with your business. One is not better than the other. We women need to stop pretending we can indeed have it all in every area of our lives at the same time. Instead, we need to get real with the life we have chosen to live. Can we all agree to stop feeling guilty if we are not able to give 100 percent to everything, but rather to celebrate that we are doing the best we can with the time, resources and energy we have been given?

In Love with the Person in the Mirror

Being in love with the person in the mirror isn't always easy. From the first half of this book you have likely come to understand that the mirror and I haven't always been friends. This was especially true after the run-in with the wicked little child in Target who called me the ugliest woman she has ever seen. On most days, I would say I am in "like" with the person in the mirror. Some days she and I are in love with each other; other days we should be on time out. I spend plenty of time trying to decide if my jeans are indeed making me look fat or if my boobs are pouring out from my dress. I would gather that most women struggle with those situations from time to time. What a difference it has made since the mirror and I have made a truce, and we have decided we will say only nice things to each other going forward.

One of the most important things I did to make myself love the girl in the mirror was to pay a professional photographer to take new headshots of me. If you have never had a professional photo shoot, you should make the investment. If you don't have the money, lean on your concierge circle and see if a friend would take great photos of you. Everyone knows someone who thinks he or she is Annie Leibovitz. I made an appointment with a super-talented photographer in San Diego. She and I walked her urban neighborhood for the perfect locations. I didn't want the photos to be too posed and stiff. The suit jacket in front of the gray background, head slightly cocked with friendly eyes, might work well for some, but this girl was not trying to be corporate. If my business is all about having fun, my headshots needed to reflect that. I was delighted to have found a photographer who honored my wish and saw the value of getting me out of the vanilla studio and into the colorful world. Helene took hundreds of photos of me that day. We wandered from brick wall to wood fence and sat on curbs to find the perfect backdrop for my headshots. What resulted was a set of photos that were not only fun but also very much a reflection of my personality. I wasn't trying to be anyone else. Helene didn't want the photos to be staged; instead, she wanted to capture the essence of my personality and to showcase my beauty. It's easy to think the photographer makes you look beautiful because of a good photo, but any photographer will tell you he or she can only work with the subject at hand. Helene is a tremendous photographer, but I had to be open to giving her something great to work with.

I sat at her Mac computer and looked at hundreds of photos she took of me. Instead of feeling like I was critical of every line, every smile, and every hair out of place, what I found instead was the spirit of who I am. I love to laugh; she captured that. I love to smile; she clicked at just the right time. I am happy in my business; she took the perfect photo. A photo shoot that could have been anxiety-producing was instead an invitation to look at myself through a different lens. These photos, which were intended to be my professional headshots, have become more of a rallying cry for me. My parents made a collage of these photos that occupies a prominent place on their wall—good parents do that. Subsequently, I have looked at these photos a great deal. There hasn't ever been one time that I looked at the photos and said, "You are the ugliest girl I have ever seen." Take that, you little devil child at Target! You may have won the battle years ago, but you have not won the war.

Now that you have your concierge circle established, why not ask a local photographer if he or she would be interested in doing a photo shoot day for your group? The photographer might offer you a reduced rate if you are willing to guarantee a certain number of subjects. Think of how much fun you would have with all your girlfriends having an afternoon of playing with the camera. The photographer would probably welcome the opportunity to gain clients in the same location versus having to drive all over town. If you don't ask the photographer to get involved, you'll never know!

One of the best advertising campaigns I have seen in a very long time is the Dove campaign for Real Beauty. The Dove brand is trying to challenge the stereotypes women have of themselves and to help them to embrace their authentic beauty. "In 2010, Dove evolved the campaign and launched an unprecedented effort to make beauty a source of confidence, not anxiety, with the Dove Movement for Self-Esteem."[1] In recent months, Dove has launched a new video called "Dove Real Beauty Sketches." If you haven't taken time to watch this video, please do yourself a favor. I promise it's three minutes you won't regret.

The premise of the video is that when women are asked to describe themselves, we often see the negative or what we deem to be the unattractive. Dove hired an FBI sketch artist and asked the women, sitting on the other side of the curtain to him, to describe their face so he could sketch their image based solely on how they described themselves. He never saw their faces, but rather made sketches based

1   See http://www.dove.us.

on their personal descriptions. All the participants were then paired up and were asked to spend some quality time together.

Fast forward a few hours, and the pairs were asked to describe the other person. From behind the curtain, Sandy had to describe Julie. When Julie was describing herself, she would use words like "huge forehead, big nose, lots of wrinkles around the eyes, unkempt hair." In contrast, when Sandy described Julie, she used statements like "petite nose, subtle laugh lines, pretty shoulder-length hair, which covers most of her forehead." The language was radically different.

The sketch artist then showed each person both images; the one he sketched from her own description, and the other from the direction of her partner. To a woman, the images by her own description were heavier, darker, and less lively. The second sketches showed lightness, a sparkle in their eyes, and a friendliness that was not present in the first image. This is some of the most powerful video I have ever seen, and I am delighted that so many women are now sharing this campaign via social media and in personal emails to each other. Kudos to Dove!

What this exercise teaches us is that for many women, how we view our own beauty is highly distorted. If others describe us as light, friendly, and full of life, how come we can't allow ourselves to live that truth? What I think is particularly important about this video is that Dove uses women to describe each other. Let's be honest; when we dress up, it's rarely for the men. It's really to try to look as good as or better than the woman sitting next to us. Men will tell you that all day long.

My good friend Alex, who is about the most direct, unemotional, and honest man-person you will meet, once said to me: "Besides underwear and shoes, we could really care less what women are wearing. Her shoes help us to imagine what she is wearing under that dress." If that's the truth, why are the XX chromosomes making such a fuss?

Alex and I met a few years ago when we were both speaking at a conference. We are about as opposite as you could find; his work focuses on world issues, while I spend my days trying to find a life size cut out of Barry Manilow or inquiring how to hire a camel for an upcoming event. We are opposites, and we view life through very different eyes. Little did we know at a conference a few years ago that we would meet and become fast friends.

Since that time, Alex has become that all-important male voice for me. We talk a lot about business. His male perspective is very valuable when I need to make a decision, submit a proposal, or consider a new project. When I need to know what guys are really thinking, both in a bar and around the boardroom table, I ask him. When I don't understand their behavior, he sets me straight. When I can't make sense of why men are so simple at times, he reminds me that I'm overthinking everything. I need a friend like Alex in my life to remind me that beauty comes in all shapes and sizes and not all men are attracted to the waif-thin models who exist on celery and chai tea. The reality he offers is hugely important to helping me to be friends with the girl in the mirror.

Be healthy, be happy, and be confident—that is the recipe for loving yourself. (Oh, and wear sexy shoes and underwear—apparently that's all the men really care about anyway. You'll feel fabulous!)

In Love with Working Hard but Playing Harder

We all know life is short. As I am writing this chapter, it happens to be the week the bombing took place at the Boston Marathon and the manhunt that ensued. Two terrorists crippled a city in fear for five days and later discovered that Boston was the wrong city to pick on. Did you hear the comedian Conan O'Brien at the Correspondents' Dinner a few days after the bombing? He made a great comment: "In Boston, nine out of ten people are related to a cop!" Truly, Boston was the wrong city to attack! When something like the bombings in

Boston happen, it should serve as a great reminder that life can change in an instant. Are you living the life you want?

I founded a global event, travel, and lifestyle concierge firm because I wanted our clients to work hard but play harder. You need not look any further than a law firm to find a community of people who work far too hard and have very little time to play. My experience at the law firm convinced me that there had to be more than just working for the billable hour. I'm not afraid of working hard; in fact, since starting my own business, I have worked much harder than I ever have. I spend fifty to sixty hours a week in my professional life. I realize that by becoming an entrepreneur, I committed to this lifestyle. However, what I didn't commit to was living a life without recess.

Several years ago, I had a conversation with my niece, Elyse, when she was heading into the fifth grade. This chat would end up having a profound effect on my business:

Me: "School starts next week. Are you excited?"

Elyse: "Yes, I can't wait to get back to recess."

Me: "Why do you like recess so much?"

Elyse: "Because I'm the wall ball champ, and it's fun to beat the boys."

Me: "I loved recess when I was in school. It was so much fun."

Elyse: "Yup, and it gives your brain a rest from all the hard work we have to do."

For whatever reason, that conversation with Elyse really resonated with me. I got to thinking about her older brother Ian, who was in seventh grade at the time, and I knew he didn't have recess scheduled into his middle school day. Certainly as adults, we no longer hear a bell ring during the day that gives us permission to go out and play. So essentially, our society is set up so you get to play for only the first six years of school, and then you spend the rest of your life dreaming of days gone by on the playground. All work and no play makes for a very dull day! My conversation with Elyse, which was at first just an innocent chat, has become the fuel behind my company philosophy. I don't want to be in a world where recess is something we talk about in terms of "remember when ..." but rather as a lifestyle we adapt. Recess was the award we earned after working hard in reading circles, after math quizzes and learning our history. Why are we no longer rewarding ourselves?

The Henley Company is committed to helping our clients to carve out time for more recess. By managing their busy lives, we can give them back the gift of time. I get it; not everyone has the ability to live a life with that much balance. Allow me to reintroduce here the concept of concierge circles. Why aren't we leaning on each other more so we can find time to play? Help is not just a four-letter word! I would argue we don't give ourselves permission because it feels too much like a luxury we don't deserve. If you could start to approach life like a co-operative effort instead of a silo, I'm convinced you would have more time to play, and life would be far more fun. I don't think when Hillary Clinton said "it takes a village" she really intended to give the village an expiration date of eighteen years. It's bogus to think that once the kids turn eighteen, the village goes into foreclosure. Instead, the village has an obligation to help smart, contributing members of society become successful regardless of their age.

In a 2012 blog post for *Entrepreneur* magazine, Richard Branson said it best:

To be refreshed and ready for anything, you need to find time for play. You are far more likely to succeed if you are having fun, so play just as hard as you work, if not harder! Find time to laugh, whether it is catching up with friends, chatting with new people, or sharing a joke on Twitter. Then when opportunity knocks, open the door and make every second count.

When was the last time you called your office and told them you were taking a *well* day rather than a sick day? Unless I was on my deathbed, I would hardly ever take a sick day, because I would much rather spend a day off enjoying recess than lying around with the sniffles. A well day probably feels too luxurious for most. You might wonder: *What would the boss say if he or she actually caught me at a museum between 9 a.m. and 5 p.m.?* If Richard Branson were your boss, he would probably give you a fist bump.

There is a ton of scientific research that supports the importance of taking a break from hard work. Play does a body and mind good—not just the organized activities like going to the gym and team sports. I'm talking about the escape from the norm: Such an escape might include painting ceramics with kindergartners during the middle of the workday, taking a language class, or even flower arranging. Whatever it is that will take you from a place of concentration to a place of meditation is important. My family believes in having great experiences. For us, experiences lead to stories that are shared around my parents' dining table on a Sunday night with many bottles of wine.

Several years ago, we implemented the monthly family experience. The rules were simple: the activity had to be something all members of the family could participate in (at the time my niece was six and my dad was turning sixty), it could not be expensive, and it had to be something none of us had ever done in San Diego. On the surface, these rules seemed limiting, but in the end we had more than enough options. Each month, a different family member was the experience captain, and it was that person's job to plan the activity. Over the years, we have participated in everything from trapeze school, to fishing on a lake, to playing Frisbee golf, to having a behind-the-scenes tour of an animal shelter.

The activity, although always fun, is secondary to the commitment we make as a family to spend time together. Your life has a start and stop date; the hyphen in between is just the series of stories you string together. The more you play, the more stories you can create. Never mind what joy and laughter it brings to the family dynamic. If you are looking for a way to incorporate play into your life, why not make it a family affair? Kids are far more invested if you give them the responsibility of planning. You can even think beyond your family; what about your neighbors? The possibilities for your concierge circle are endless!

In Love with the People You Surround Yourself With

I devoted a whole chapter to talking about the people you have chosen to surround yourself with. Have you identified your basement dwellers and your penthouse party people yet? I purposefully use the verb *choose* because it is indeed a choice. Being related to someone is not an excuse for feeling like that person has to be a barnacle on your life. Every day you wake up, you have a choice of how you are going to spend your day and with whom you spend it. Choose wisely!

Never have the people I surround myself with been more important and significant to me than the last few years. In those crucial years, I was dealing with a shattered heart, depression, starting a business, and financial insecurity. My family was the rock I needed to get through my daily struggles. Equally as important were the small but mighty group of friends I held onto tightly. There is plenty of research that highlights the importance of social interaction. It's good not only for our psyche but also for our health. A 2010 *Forbes* article, highlights the importance of social relationships:

Turns out, social isolation may actually be one of the biggest risk factors for human mortality. As an example, here is how the study corresponds low social interaction to some of the more common risks to our wellbeing:

>> As bad for your health as smoking fifteen cigarettes a day.

>> As dangerous as being an alcoholic.

>> As harmful as never exercising.

>> Twice as dangerous as obesity.[2]

While I was recently helping a friend through a difficult personal situation, she made a comment that I've always found significant: "I never really knew who my real friends were until this happened. I realized that I needed to clean house, and those that have stuck by me are the measure of true friends. As hard as it is to lose friends, the silver lining in this situation is that I don't have to keep pretending and feeling like I have to fit in. I was tired of living an unauthentic life. I no longer feel like a stranger in my own life."[3]

Diane made a choice that greatly impacted her family: she started an affair with her neighbor. I purposefully don't use the word *mistake* because nothing about the situation was an accident. They were two consenting adults who mutually agreed to pursue a relationship while being married to other people. Miscounting the number of forks you need to set the table is a mistake. An affair is a choice. Let's not pretend it's anything else. However, thousands of innocent acts eventually lead to two people having an affair. Diane did not wake up one day and randomly decide she would cheat on her husband. Instead, everything

2   See http://www.forbes.com/2010/08/24/health-relationships-longevity-forbes-woman-well-being-social-isolation.html.

3   Paraphrased from Diane (not her real name).

in her life had led up to the day she and the neighbor, Kirk, decided to start both an emotional and physical relationship. They both got a case of the "weak knees and can't help its," as my mom would say.

For Diane, deep in the back of her mind, the affair was an attempt to be validated. She admits that throughout her life, she has always been the "good girl" and the rule-follower. Fast-forward to her forties, and this pattern manifested itself into needing attention and approval. She started to hear what she needed from Kirk. She gravitated to someone who provided something she was lacking. My own personal opinion is that Kirk's libido and ego told her exactly what she needed to hear. If this is true, then it becomes difficult to identify a distinction between a conscious choice and an unresolved subconscious issue for Diane. We could have hours of conversation about the morality issue, and whether or not to label Diane and Kirk as bad people. That's not relevant to this topic. Instead, what seemed like the worst thing that could happen to her family ultimately ended up being the best of circumstances.

Diane called me in tears a few years ago to tell me that her husband had discovered the affair because Kirk's wife had found emails between them. I'm hardly perfect, and it's not my position to judge, so instead of branding her with the scarlet letter, I asked her where she was planning on staying that night. For two weeks, Diane slept on my couch. The friend I had laughed with on plenty of occasions and shared plenty of wine with was now crying hysterically in my tiny apartment. Not only did she question if she would ever be able to repair the damage she had done to her family but she also felt the overriding shame the neighborhood had cast upon her. She was broken in every possible way a woman could be, and all I could do was try to make her feel safe and supported.

It was fascinating to watch how the community responded to the situation. Last time I checked, it took two to have an affair. She was perceived to be a home-wrecker and shameful. However, when people would talk about Kirk, he would not be cast in the same light. It was sort of the shrug-of-the-shoulders and "boys will be boys" mentality. Few doubted this was the first time he had strayed.

Why did the neighborhood perceive Kirk to be less at fault than Diane? Probably because of the preconceived belief that good women don't do that sort of thing. Kirk's wife was perceived to be the ultimate victim in the whole situation. By contrast, people seemed to feel sorry for Diane's husband, Neil, because he was married to the home-wrecker. This whole situation was rampant with double standards.

Diane and Neil worked painstaking hours on their marriage. Most important, they both took a lot of time to work on themselves. Diane realized that the women she had called friends, those that had come to her house for Bunko parties and fellow moms she would see at her children's school, were indeed fair-weather friends. When the going got tough, they immediately became basement dwellers. It was easier to judge Diane than to look at their own relationships.

I know plenty about what was happening on their street; let's just say the TV show *Desperate Housewives* could have been filmed there. There were many living in glass houses who should not have thrown stones. The amount of name-calling, talking behind Diane's back, and judgment that came from this breaking news story on the street was shocking. I guess it is easy to poke fun of someone else's wrongdoing than to work on our own lives! Ironically, most of these women who judged considered themselves churchgoers. Last time I checked, judgment wasn't a virtue that was preached in the church at the end of their road.

What has happened in the five years since this incident has been significant. I could not be more proud of Diane and Neil, and I am also proud to still call them my friends. They turned a negative situation into a positive outcome. They spent hours in therapy together. They learned how to communicate, and they chose to fall back in love with each other after too many years of taking each other for granted. They also realized who their real friends are, and no longer feel they have to placate the false friends who are only there for the wine. They even went so far as to move a couple streets over from the *Desperate Housewives* neighborhood because they wanted a fresh start. They deserved that.

Kirk and his wife stayed in the same neighborhood, and few know if they have done the work to move from existing to thriving in their marriage. For their children's sake, I hope they have.

Diane has remarked on several occasions what a relief it is to no longer be keeping up with the Joneses, but she doesn't mean monetarily. Keeping up with the Joneses (or should we say the Kardashians now?) can be mentally draining and emotionally exhausting. Diane was always trying to fit in and to be liked. This carries over from her childhood of always wanting to be included. What you don't handle in your childhood always finds you in your adulthood—the truth cannot hide forever. Diane's need to be accepted by the so-called friends in their neighborhood eventually manifested itself in an affair with Kirk. If you seek attention, eventually you will find it—even where you aren't supposed to.

Although her circle of friends is now smaller than ever, Diane has the most authentic friendships she has ever had in her life. She is now truly in love with the people around her—no more basement dwellers allowed. She holds her head high, knowing that her marriage and friendships are stronger than ever. The affair is one chapter in her life; it doesn't need to define her. It certainly changed her, but in a positive way after a lot of very hard work and forgiveness. Surrounding herself with those who don't cast judgment helped both her and Neil to move forward to a powerful position. She gave herself permission to forgive herself and to clean house of her so-called friends. Good for her.

In Love with Yourself More Than Anyone Else

It might not be popular with some, but I'm giving you permission to be selfish from this day forward. I'm not talking about being superior to everyone else or demanding that you get the biggest piece of cake when it's cut. Rather, I'm talking about putting your personal happiness above anyone else's. If you're always trying to make your partner, your kids, or your friends happy, how is there any time for you? You can't live an authentic life if you are at the service of everyone else. You may disagree with me and think this premise is too self-serving, but I would like to challenge your opinion.

In my relationships with both Colin and Jack, I put their happiness and their needs above my own. By trying to be everything to them, I lost sight of who Nicole was, and this self-neglect had an emotional, physical, and mental effect on me. Had I loved myself enough in both those relationships, I would not have stood for Colin's temper or Jack's cheating and lying ways. I gave them more of me than I gave myself, and where did that get me? Nowhere but Broken Heart Alley.

I never set boundaries to define for them what I was unwilling to put up with. Instead, I blurred the line between self-worth and subservience. If loving them enough didn't make them better people in our relationship, I at least owed it to myself to be the best person I could be. For far too many years, I failed at that, which is why I will never say that I was a victim in those relationships. I *chose* to stay, and I *allowed* them to treat me the way they did. I'm as much to blame as they are because I didn't let my architect speak up. I'm not trying to be a martyr, but to fail to acknowledge my contribution in these relationships is foolish. Distance from both of these men has taught me that I failed myself miserably when I conceded to loving them more than I loved myself. I was blinded by love, but that's only an excuse for so long. My little architect had finally had enough of me not loving myself, so she opened my mouth and let my heart speak in both relationships. It's not always easy, but I had to give myself permission to be selfish enough to get out. Otherwise, I was going to be swallowed up in service to both of them.

I also had to give myself permission to work on the part of my psyche that is initially attracted to narcissistic men. They are always exciting in the beginning but have no capacity to change. Eventually, when you know better, you do better.

Make Your Own Magic

Several years ago, an event colleague told me about a gift she had given her sixteen-year-old niece. She believed that every woman had to know she could make her own magic, so she made a personalized, bedazzled wand as a graduation present. I absolutely love this idea. I've used it both as a gift and as a project for a women's organization I once cofounded. I have my magic wand proudly displayed on my desk, and I look at it every day for inspiration. I believe strongly that you have to make your own magic; you can't rely on any person, place, or thing to bring you happiness. So grab your wand and join me for the next few chapters, where we are going to talk about how you can create your own opportunities and start designing the life you want to live! Sprinkle your pixie dust now!

Ask Yourself

Are you in love with your business? If not, what would you rather be doing?

Are you in love with the person in the mirror? If not, why?

When is the last time you allowed yourself to take time to play? What's holding you back? What family or neighborhood experiences could you implement?

Are you in love with the people you surround yourself with? If not, what changes should you make?

Are you ready to start making your own magic? How will you start?

CHAPTER NINE
The Big Ask

Don't live life as a spectator. Always examine life. Espouse new ideas.
Long for new things, constantly discovering new interests, escaping from
boring routines. Engage life with enthusiasm—grasping life aggressively
and squeezing from it every drop of excitement, satisfaction, and joy.
The key to unleashing life's potential is attitude.
—Felix "Fearless" Baumgarnter, daredevil sky diver

ONE OF THE GREATEST HIGHLIGHTS OF MY LIFE WAS
the months I spent back in 2000 working as a consultant on a project
near London. In May of 2000, I completed my master's degree from
the University of San Diego. At the time, I was working at USD as the
assistant director of Alumni Relations. I could not have been more
grateful to have had the opportunity to work at USD as a young
professional. I was responsible for the event portfolio for the alumni
of the university, as well as the stewardship of the volunteers and
alumni board. I had the pleasure of working for a great man, Trif,
who was the director of Alumni Relations, and the honorary mayor
on campus. Trif had a relatively young staff with all of us being freshly
out of college. However, that didn't stop him from giving us a ton
of autonomy and responsibility. Trif's philosophy was you learn by

doing, so go do, and he would be our safety net if we fell. That was an unbelievable gift for a twenty-three-year-old working at her first real job with great benefits. I look back fondly on my days at USD and give Trif a lot of credit for taking a chance on me.

As part of my benefits package, USD offered employees the opportunity to earn a degree, so I took advantage of my educational gift and started my master's program in educational leadership. As I was finishing my studies and nearing graduation, I started to do some soul searching. As much as I loved my position at USD, I felt after nearly five years that my career had run its course. I had never taken advantage of a study-abroad program, so I figured it was a good time to make up for lost experiences.

Since I had family living in England and had a general love of all things British, I set my sights on the mighty UK. My authentic intention was to land a job in the UK so I could work and live there for an extended period of time. I wasn't interested in being just a tourist; I wanted to be completely entrenched in the experience. But how? It's not like you can just pick up and move to England without a job—not legally, anyhow! And at the time, Prince William wasn't old enough to marry, so my chances of getting a work permit through marriage were slim. I doubt the Queen would approve of an American cougar.

I started to share my dream of living and working in England with anyone who cared to listen. During this period of pontification, my mom happened to go to Las Vegas for a conference. While she was there, she met a man named Nigel, who worked for Pfizer in Sandwich, England. Yes, there is such a place. She took his business card and tucked it away. Within a few weeks, I was once again championing my UK cause when my mom remembered meeting Nigel. She gave me his business card and told me to contact him to let him know that I was looking for work in the UK. Like that was going to work—some random guy she meets in Vegas is going to be my ticket to England? Yeah, right! Knowing that every lead might eventually lead somewhere, I sent an email to Nigel, the stranger.

Hi Nigel,

My name is Nicole Matthews, and I live in San Diego, California. My mom, Brenda, recently met you at a conference you were attending in Las Vegas. Please forgive me for being so forward, but I am currently seeking employment opportunities in the UK. I have extensive experience in event management and am just finishing my master's degree in educational leadership at the University of San Diego. Might you know of any companies that could benefit from my skills and experience? I have attached my résumé for your review. Thank you in advance for your consideration.

I pushed Send and figured it would end up in his spam folder. To my surprise, Nigel the stranger became Nigel the miracle-worker. He was very kind when he responded to my email a few days later:

Hi Nicole,

Thank you for your email. It was nice to meet your mum in Las Vegas. It looks like you have a lot of strong experience. Unfortunately, at the moment, Pfizer does not have any opportunities for international workers, but I am a member of the UK Recreational Council, a professional organization for all directors who oversee corporate wellness programs at large UK businesses. I will be happy to pass your CV along to my colleagues for their review. Please keep me posted on your progress.

I was excited and deeply appreciated that Nigel had not marked my email as junk and actually took the time to respond. Let's hear it for my mom and the random business card!

As much as I appreciated Nigel's efforts, I really wasn't that optimistic that my mission would get much further down the path. That is, of course, until several weeks later when an email popped into my inbox:

Hi Nicole,

I was given your CV from Nigel at Pfizer. My name is Tony King, and I am the director of the Prudential Ibis Club in Reading, England. I have read your CV with interest and would love to discuss an opportunity for you to consult with my company. Our club serves the employees of Prudential Insurance. We are currently undergoing an overhaul on our meeting and event space and would welcome your insight on how we could improve our programming. Additionally, your degree in leadership would be beneficial as I am trying to reorganize the team. Might you have time for us to speak by phone about creating the opportunity? I look forward to speaking with you at your convenience.

Might we have time to speak? I was dialing 011 44, the country code for England as I was reading the email. Could this be possible? Had my authentic intention really started to manifest itself?

Tony and I started an email exchange, which eventually led to a phone call. This was back in 2000, long before you could google just about anyone—for instance, the sex offender registry and the crime logs. Although Tony's voice was charming and very British on the other end of the phone, I really had very little information about the man that was giving me the great opportunity I had asked for.

On September 23, 2000, my parents drove me to LAX and put me on a plane to London. Eleven hours later, I stood in the flurry of Heathrow Airport, wearing a dark blue University of San Diego sweatshirt, and waited for a man to walk up to me and ask, "Are you Nicole Matthews?" My response was, "I hope you are Tony King." It indeed was Tony, and my great adventure was about to begin. It felt like a scene out of a movie. Now I know how the mail-order brides feel when they make the journey to start a new life.

Properly dressed in his tweed jacket with pocket square, Tony developed a sweat as he tried to load this American's luggage into his midsize car. Luckily, he used the pink pocket square to dab his brow. Somehow, short of tying it to the roof of the car, we got the luggage puzzle to fit.

The day was perfectly English; the gray weather mirrored by the gray color of his four-door Vauxhall. My jet lag faded away as Tony toured me around the small villages and towns, including Henley-on-Thames, as we made our way to Reading. I will never forget David Gray's song, *Babylon*, playing from the radio as we crossed the bridge over the Thames and drove into Henley. The first chorus of *Babylon* played as we passed The Angel on the Bridge pub and the drizzle of rain started to fall. Everything looked foreign, although I felt very much at home.

Tony King was in his late fifties when we first met. He had floppy brown hair and suaveness about him that is a combination of a dapper Englishman and a renaissance man. He had a boisterous laugh, and I would later learn that he danced like John Travolta, at least in his own mind. Tony was a party all rolled into one.

Tony took a nervous young American girl in her late twenties, living outside of the country for the first time, and made sure she was properly taken care of from the very minute she landed. On the first day, he had arranged three different flats for me to consider for residence, and shortly thereafter hired a car for the length of my stay. He took his obligation of taking care of this Yankee Doodle with all seriousness. I chose to live with the son of one of Tony's personal assistants, a young man by the name of Paul, who was tall, sporty, and had a head of ginger-red hair. Our modern flat was in the center of Reading and provided easy walking distance to the town and shopping. Paul's flat was on the ground level of the building, and although it was quite spacious and well equipped, it did present one problem: mold growing on my shoes. You see, in England it rains a little ... or a lot! The year I lived there it rained more than it had in two hundred years. I felt like Noah piloting his ark every time I hit the road.

One day, as I was getting ready for work, I pulled a pair of shoes out from under my dresser. With the amount of luggage I had brought with me, you can imagine how it was to put my belongings in every nook and cranny of my small room. Remember, I came to England with three suitcases, and most English closets are big enough for only a small carry-on bag! I pulled out a pair of black flats from under the wardrobe and realized they were covered in green fur. Confused, I took a closer look and realized that the fur was actually mold. This was extremely perplexing to a San Diego native who barely owns an umbrella due to the number of perfect seventy-five-degree days we regularly enjoy. The combination of being on the ground floor, along with the flooding rain, had left the flat continuously damp. My shoes fell victim to the dampness. I had to brush off the mold and squish my way to the office that day.

To say that I worked hard at the Prudential Ibis Club is really an exaggeration. Let's be honest; I spent the mornings reading the UK papers and taking turns putting the kettle on for the morning brew. By lunchtime, I was behind the bar in the pub, pulling pints for the conference center attendees. By the end of the day, I was reviewing their event portfolio and engaging with staff. I look back fondly on those easy days since I now have fifty-hour weeks. Part of my responsibility was to infiltrate the staff so that I could give Tony an accurate pulse on who was happy, who was efficient, and who needed to find the door. The only way to do that effectively was to get as friendly as possible.

One highlight of the trip was my family flying over for Thanksgiving dinner. Due to the loss of the colonies, that's not really a big holiday for the British, but Tony made sure it was special for us. His wife was a caterer, so she researched the menu of a typical Thanksgiving dinner. My family and I spent our Thanksgiving that year at a beautiful dining room table in Tony and Jill's thatched cottage. The cottage, with its singing beams and fireplace large enough to stand up in, was built in the 1300s. This thatched cottage was four hundred years older than the oldest holiday we celebrate as a country. To say that the Thanksgiving of 2000 was special is an understatement.

This is just another example of how Tony became my guardian angel during my trip. How do you ever thank the person that single-handedly made your authentic intention a reality? I've tried several times since then, but it never feels like there are words that can convey my deepest appreciation. We need to craft a word that means mega-thank-you times a thousand!

Late in December, as I sat in my damp flat, working on Paul's computer with dial-up Internet service and the shrieking that came with every connection, I wrote a comprehensive analysis of my time at the Prudential. Tony had asked for my suggestions, recommendations, and insight. I typed as once again the rain fell on the window and Enya played from the stereo. The gray weather mirrored the heaviness in my heart as I realized my time in the UK was coming to the end. The work visa I was able to obtain entitled me to stay in the country through December 23. It was with much sadness that I boarded the plane on that day, toting all seven suitcases. (The shopping in the UK is very good!) I watched as my plane climbed altitude over Windsor Castle and over Reading. As I physically traveled west, I knew my heart would always have a place in England. This defining chapter of my life had come to an end.

It's easy to be sad given the relatively short amount of time I was able to spend working in the UK, but there is no reason to be anything less than elated. Nine months before I had set my intention to work abroad, and thanks to a rogue business card from Las Vegas, the dream became a reality. Why? Because I asked for the chance. If I waited for a job opportunity in London to come knock on my door, I would still be waiting. Instead, I set my intention and made it happen. If you don't ask for what you want, the answer will always be no. So why not ask? You have nothing to lose! I give you permission to just start asking!

By the time I was twenty-eight years old, creating my own opportunities had led to an amazing internship and a consulting gig in London. I knew I was on to something, and I was never going to see life the same way again. Although I had an incredible support system around me, in the end, the sole reason I was going to be a success or failure would be my effort. That was a powerful lesson for me. It has continued to serve me well to this day. Figure out what you want to do with your life, set your intention, and then start asking for help. It's the only way to move from dreaming to doing.

In July of 2005, as I watched the news, I was delighted to learn that London had been selected as the host city for the 2012 Olympic Games. My authentic intention spoke up and told me that I was going to figure out a way to work those games. As an event professional and a sports lover, to me the Olympics have always been the Holy Grail—the ultimate project to work on. I had seven years to put the plan into motion and turn the dream into reality. Remember, once you set your authentic intention, you've determined your destination. Then, it's just up to your internal GPS to start the journey.

For a few years, I poked around on Olympics websites and international job boards hoping the perfect opportunity would fall into my lap. I'm not sure why I figured that was going to be the way, since every good thing before had come from me creating the opportunity for myself. As the years clicked on toward 2012, I became more anxious about landing a job that would allow me to work the games. I continued to work my dream.

I was working at my desk one Sunday evening back in November of 2011. Suddenly, with a moment of inspiration, I found myself typing an email:

From: Nicole Matthews
Subject: Working London 2012
Date: November 13, 2011 4:53:07 PM PST
To: Nicole Matthews
Bcc: Undisclosed Recipients

Friends,

I'm a big believer that you have to put your "ask" out into the world so the universe knows how to help you! So here's my ask ... I'm looking for any leads to connect with companies who have the ability to hire Americans to work the Olympic Games. I'm most interested in working the London 2012 games next summer. It's a dream of mine to work for them! Given my love of the UK, the London Games is a perfect fit. I'm fairly open to any position that would get me there, but obviously with my extensive experience in event management, marketing, strategic partnership, and concierge work, it would be great if I could utilize my skill set.

Any introductions you could make on my behalf would be deeply appreciated! If I can ever return the favor, please let me know!

Cheers,
Nicole

I sent the email out to more than a hundred people in my sphere; the only criterion I used was that they would know my name when the email landed in their inbox. They didn't have to be my best friend; they just needed to know of me. I pushed Send once again on an email that would change my life. I knew that someone knew someone who knew someone who could help me get to the Olympics. I was counting on six degrees of Kevin Bacon!

Within three days, over twenty-five people responded to my email. I thought that was an astonishing rate of return. The email responses had suggestions on who I could contact: "My cousin works in London, I'll reach out to her," said one email. "Our company has an office in London, I'll check with the HR department there," said another. And "my friend worked the Vancouver Games; I'll connect the two of you," came yet another response. I was overwhelmed.

The email had done two things for me: First, it created an incredible positive swell of good energy in the universe to help me achieve my goal. Second, it became the all-important measure of accountability for me. People now knew about my goal and they were indeed going to ask if I had yet achieved it. All over town, people would ask, "Do you have a job at the Olympics yet?" With that much positive energy, I could just feel myself getting closer to my dream. Their interest in my goal was a great motivator.

My big break finally came when I was talking to a fellow professor I teach with at the community college. She had worked numerous Olympic Games, so I quickly told her about my intention. Had I not found that twenty seconds of courage to plead my case and let her know what my architect was designing for my life, I would never have landed in London. Jan made a very important introduction for me to an international event firm focused on worldwide sporting events. I will call this company WorldWide Events. This was the closest I had come to connecting with the right company. Several weeks went by, and I heard nothing. Jan was kind enough to follow up with WorldWide Events and encouraged them to contact me. With less than six months left before that tiny little event called the Olympics, you can imagine how busy they were in the office. Persistence paid off, however, and in late February, I had my first phone interview with the WorldWide Events program director in the London office. This was one of the biggest interviews of my life. All of my Olympic eggs were in one basket, and I couldn't blow this opportunity. I spent over an hour on the phone with Lynn in London, and we seemed to hit it off. I felt cautious with every answer, wanting to come across as professional, enthusiastic, and well experienced.

The first interview went very well, and Lynn invited me for a second interview via Skype. I was getting closer. A few weeks later, I Skyped the WorldWide Events office and spoke with Lynn together with Claudia, the account executive managing the program to which I was going to be assigned. I spoke a lot about my vast event experience, and the fact that I had previous experience working in London. I also understood the program would include many high-level VIPs, so I referred heavily to my concierge experience and how we regularly work with high-profile executives. The interview went well from my perspective, but I knew the ball was definitely in their court. The waiting was a killer.

It was ironic that I was substitute teaching at the community college when the good news came. A colleague at the community college had made the introduction to WorldWide Events for me, so the timing was perfect when I checked my email at the class break and found the offer letter. At first, when I read the email I could barely comprehend the subject line: "Offer Letter—London 2012 Olympics." One email literally changed my life. I picked up my phone and started speed-dialing my parents but to no avail; they picked a fine time to be busy! My next call was to my sister Jodi, and I could barely get the words out before we both started crying. My authentic intention had come to fruition. Jodi could not be more thrilled for me, and I heard her telling my niece, Elyse the great news. As I was talking to Jodi, I could hear the text message alert on my phone dinging. My little Elyse sent the best text message ever:

> I am sooooo proud of u Titi. I knew u could do it and
> ur hard work pays off.
> I love u <3!

One of the proudest days of my life was attending the going-away party my parents threw for me before I left for London. My closest friends and family gathered to celebrate my impending great adventure. Everyone in attendance knew that my intention was to end up in London, and their support helped me to turn my dream into a reality. These were my penthouse party people. When I left for London, I not only felt excitement for what was to come, but I also felt obligated to enjoy every minute of the experience because I knew that most people would never earn this opportunity. My party people were going to live vicariously through me, and I wanted to make sure I did them proud.

For seven weeks, I worked in London and had the experience of a lifetime. I was fortunate because I was given a tremendous responsibility in my role with WorldWide Events. This allowed me to have access to a unique Olympic experience. London was never more beautiful, and I couldn't love my craft of event management any more than the very long days I worked on the Olympic project. I was directly responsible for VIP management and event planning for one of the top Olympic sponsors. In my original email asking my sphere to help me to end up in London, I offered to take any position that would allow me to work the Games. The level of responsibility, access, and privilege I was given blew me away. Quite simply, I was incredibly lucky. I recognize that my Olympic experience was special. Be careful what you wish for; reality might actually blow away your dreams.

Had I never asked for the opportunity to intern with the event planning company, or asked Nigel at Pfizer if there was an opportunity to work abroad, or asked my sphere to help me to find a position to work the Olympics, none of these intentions would have come true. The difference between dreams and reality is action, and part of the action requires you to make the *big ask!* It's one thing to just wish and hope that one day your dream will come true, but quite another to actually put energy and effort into making your dream a reality. The only difference between you and me is the amount of action I put into setting my authentic intention and then making it happen. I promise I am not better than you in any way. I'm not particularly special. It's just a matter of giving myself permission to accomplish what I have set out to do.

You may recall that in October 2012, "Fearless" Felix Baumgartner stepped off a capsule hoisted by a giant helium balloon nearly 128,000 feet above New Mexico. He became the first human to break the sound barrier with only a pressurized suit. Five years before opening the capsule door and stepping off without hesitation, Baumgartner believed this feat was possible. Imagine the big ask he did when he approached Red Bull to be a sponsor of the mission. Imagine the conversation: "So, here's an idea … I'm looking to pilot an enormous helium balloon almost twenty-five miles above the earth and then step out of the capsule and become the first person to exceed the sound barrier during a free fall … are you in?" If he never would have asked, the answer would have been no. Instead, Red Bull said yes and the rest—as they say—is history.

A fun fact about Fearless Felix is that he suffered from debilitating claustrophobia, which he had to overcome in order to wear his life-saving space suit. Are you honestly going to keep telling yourself that whatever dream you are trying to make a reality is harder than what Fearless Felix had to overcome and accomplish: to successfully fall from twenty-five miles above us?

> The only thing standing between you and your goal is the bullshit story you keep telling yourself as to why you can't achieve it.
>
> —Felix Baumgartner

The time is now for you to set your intention on how you would like to design the life you want to live and then create a plan for making it become a reality. Let your inner architect speak. Figure out who is in your circle that either helps or hinders your progress, and then lean on others by asking for help. I promise, the opportunities you can create are endless.

Ask Yourself

What would be your big ask at this moment?

What Olympic-sized experiences do you want to have?

Draft an email for your big ask. What would it say?

Who can you ask to help you make your big ask come true?

CHAPTER TEN

Create Your Own Opportunities

You get in life what you have the courage to ask for.
—Oprah Winfrey

I STARTED THIS BOOK BY TALKING ABOUT THE FACT that I see the world through the lens of opportunity. As I look back at the life and career-changing moments I've had, I can directly tie my ability to create an opportunity for myself to the outcome. I preach to my students on a regular basis how important it is to be in control of your own destiny. I realize life likes to throw little hurdles our way, but eventually time heals all wounds and the world keeps turning. Look at any successful entrepreneur or someone who has made mega money; nine times out of ten they've done it by their own hands and because of their own blood, sweat, and tears. They haven't just been handed the keys to success. Even Oprah had to create opportunities when she saw the opening. Had she not been bold and brave, she might still be sitting behind a desk reading the news as a newscaster rather than becoming the self-made billionaire and mega brand she is today. I'm sure Oprah would be the first to tell you that hard work, drive, and a sense of living her best life is the fuel that moved her from a childhood of poverty into the penthouse she now calls home. Given the circumstances of where she came from, statistically speaking, Oprah should have aspired to have a "good" job, to get married, and to raise a few kids. She chose otherwise and decided that the only limitation she would put on her life was whatever existed beyond her dreams. Why can't you be the next Oprah? Is it that you aren't dreaming big enough, or you haven't yet given yourself permission to be your best self?

Throughout this book you have heard me share my stories, and those of other women, of moments when we have created opportunities. Hopefully, you took inspiration from the story of securing my first event management internship, working in Reading, asking the law firm to be a client of my new business, and, most recently, the story of my putting out the big ask and getting myself work at the London 2012 Olympics.

These can be considered one-off external experiences. I put the authentic intention out to the world, and through hard work and leaning on others, my dream became reality. Each of these moments has been important for my personal and professional growth, but creating your own opportunities does not have to be just about life-changing feats. They can be daily accomplishments. When I started to see that creating my own opportunities in my business was the key to success, I locked down the formula and began to rinse and repeat.

My first entry into creating my own opportunities came in the form of self-producing my own event. As in most industries, event professionals are taught to always chase the client. How many times have we been told to go where the client is; be what the client needs; and my favorite, "The client is always right!" Perhaps this is true. However, this much effort can be exhausting. In fact, it makes running a successful business a bit challenging. I have no interest in partaking in the networking smorgasbord du jour. I'm sure your city is no different than mine; morning, noon, and night you could be networking in San Diego. How many chicken skewers and vegetable crudités can one eat? Never mind the expense of every $25 to $50 registration fee. No thank you! I would rather sit on my couch eating chips and salsa, and watching *The Housewives of New York*. Although this is my preference, this approach does not pay my bills, so I realized that I had to start making an effort. But how? How could I turn business development into an activity that I could not only tolerate but enjoy? Simple: I became my own client!

I can already hear the naysayers questioning how becoming my own client is really good for business. I understand the multiplier effect; I know you need to introduce fresh money into the equation, or else the money runs out. So choosing to look inward versus outward almost seems contradictory for this opportunity creator who wears opportunity like a fabulous accessory. Here's how it all came to be.

Back in 2008, a tiny movie called *Sex and the City: The Movie* was about to be released. You might have heard of it! I was having coffee with my friend Alicia one morning, and we were talking about how excited we were that the movie was coming out. At this time, it had been a few years since the television show *Sex and the City* had gone off the air, so we were certainly missing our four girls: Carrie, Samantha, Charlotte, and Miranda. Don't lie; you know exactly which girl you are like!

As Alicia and I were talking about current events, she said, "You know what you should do: You should put together a big event around the opening of the movie. Why not produce a movie premier?" Hello, Captain Obvious, I forgot I was the event planner at the table. Why had I not been thinking that strategically? The hype for the upcoming movie was quickly becoming a beast of its own. I would have been foolish to miss that train.

I quickly set out to develop my own plan. The conversation with Alicia took place in February 2008; the movie was launching on May 28. Time was of the essence. I knew that I wanted this event to be a memory, not just a moment. I recognized that in order to convince people to purchase tickets I would have to create a unique occasion that they would not be able to experience on their own. Plenty of women were already planning a girls' night out, where they would go see the movie and enjoy drinks either before or after. I wanted to craft an event so rare that they would talk about it for a long time to come. My initial planning yielded three key elements. I knew I needed a place to show the movie, an after-party location, and the media.

From there, I just started asking. I wish I could say that the formula is some super-secret scientific equation, but the reality boiled down to just asking strategic partners to get involved. Most people don't have the courage to ask. That's too bad.

The most important element to asking strategic partners to get involved with your event is to first understand your target market or demographic. Without knowing who is going to be in the audience, it's tough to convince someone to get involved. I knew the *Sex and the City* generation is sophisticated, professional women in the twenty-five- to forty-five-year-old range. Therefore, when I thought about asking partners to engage, I wanted to make sure they would benefit from this audience.

Once I had solidified the concept in my own head, I paid attention to the people and companies I already knew. I made a list of key vendors and relationships I already had established. My first call tapped into a preexisting relationship I had with J Public Relations, a super-savvy and dynamic PR firm based in San Diego. JPR is a woman-owned public relations firm that in the last eight years has gone from a small San Diego firm to an internationally recognized PR powerhouse.

I had the pleasure of meeting Jamie Lynn Sigler, the founding partner of JPR, several years before. She's a trendsetter and a mover and shaker in San Diego. I was delighted to share the stage with her when we were both honored a few years ago as one of *San Diego Metro Magazine's* 40 Under 40 award recipients. I've always admired the work that J Public Relations has accomplished and had great respect for Jamie. She presents the perfect combination of style, beauty, and smarts, all balancing on the perfect pair of Jimmy Choos.

J Public Relations has a great tag line: "Don't let the pink fool you."

And I can attest that they have turned pink from a soft color into a bold statement. These girls kick PR ass and look fabulous in their stilettos while doing it.

Knowing that they specialize in hospitality, luxury, and hotel properties, it made total sense for me to try to engage JPR as a partner in my *Sex and the City* project. I reached out to their team and pitched my event concept. I asked if any of their local venue clients might be interested in being the after-party venue for the event. Jamie, along with her associate Lauren Clifford, knew that the *Sex and the City* media train had already left the station, so they were eager to position one of their clients as a partner in the San Diego movie premier event.

JPR reached out to a local nightclub called Stingaree, which back in 2008 was the hot new club in our city. Stingaree immediately took interest, and within a week of pitching my initial event concept to JPR, we were all sitting around a table at the Stingaree head office talking about the opportunity for the movie premier. Stingaree agreed to get involved and to serve as the venue partner for the after-party. This in and of itself was a home run! I finally had locked in a fabulous venue for my guests to retreat to after the movie.

In addition to securing the venue, by asking JPR to get involved, I essentially adopted a PR firm. Since JPR was the public relations firm for Stingaree, I knew that JPR would want to make sure that its client was successful, so a media campaign was drafted.

Are you starting to see how the power of partnership works? I asked JPR to reach out to their clients; they agreed and Stingaree came on board as a partner. But the bonus was working with JPR on the publicity of the event. Stingaree was very interested in getting involved because of the demographic and audience we were going to deliver. Obviously, as a nightclub, they are very interested in the twenty-five to forty-five female demographic. Of course, they would be interested in having an additional five hundred people in their venue on a Friday night buying alcohol. That was a huge motivation for them to get involved.

Once I had the after-party locked and loaded, I could concentrate on securing the movie venue. Some might think that was putting the cart before the horse. But in the movie world, movie theatre companies often make last-minute decisions on which films they will show. In the Gaslamp Quarter in downtown San Diego, there are two movie theatres. I knew that the film would not be shown at both; they are only blocks away from each other. I had to wait until about six weeks before the event, until I knew which theatre was going to be the movie house. This all has to do with how movie theatre companies buy films for showing. There is a whole formula on how it happens that is far more complex than we need to get into now. Your takeaway here is that generally speaking, two different movie theatres do not show the same films within the same neighborhood.

Unbeknown to me, public relations firms in each major market are hired by the movie distribution companies to manage movie-screening events. These take place days before the actual opening day of the movie. You've probably heard on your local radio station that they are giving away tickets to a screening of an upcoming movie. The public relations firm is hired to create interest and enthusiasm before the movie opens. The lucky ticket winners from the radio then see the movie days before the official opening. If things go right, they then become walking billboards. They tell all their friends that this is the best movie they have ever seen, and that they should rush to buy tickets.

JPR was kind enough to make an introduction on my behalf to that local public relations firm in San Diego, who are responsible for the movie screenings. Why would JPR do this? Besides the obvious fact that they are smart businesswomen, they also have their client Stingaree's best interest in mind. The more tickets we sold to the event, the more people would come through the door at Stingaree. This is the power of partnership.

When JPR endorsed me, the other PR firm took notice. I was able to work with the team to support their local efforts in promoting the movie. They produced the screening a few days before the opening weekend, so they didn't see my event as direct competition with their efforts. My relationship with the second PR firm made a huge impact because they went to New Line Cinema on my behalf and were able to obtain an endorsement for my event. New Line was impressed with what I was intending to create and, therefore, felt they didn't need to recreate the wheel in the San Diego market. With New Line Cinema's endorsement, came the official artwork for the movie and access to the official merchandise they had produced for the film. Had I never asked JPR to get involved, I'm confident that I would never have had the benefit of New Line Cinema. This is a perfect example of "If you never ask, the answer is always no!"

With the movie theatre locked in, the after-party venue secured, and the endorsement by New Line Cinema, I knew that my event now had validity, and planning was in full effect.

We are so lucky to have that little thing called the Internet. It's amazing what you can find. With a little research, I was able to obtain a list of all the product placements in the upcoming film. Reaching out to the involved companies was crucial. My pitch to them included two key elements: first, the confirmation of the after-party venue, and the endorsement of New Line Cinema; second, the demographic I was going to deliver. I was creating an environment for these products to have a live event for *Sex and the City: The Movie,* where they could showcase their product or service. This was a direct tie-in to their involvement in the movie.

I also reached out to local vendors whom I knew would also want to gain access to this specific demographic. Who said yes? I'm proud to say: SKYY Vodka, Bag Borrow or Steal, Saks Fifth Avenue, Sephora, Cricket Wireless, Hard Rock Hotel, Niemen Marcus, and Jimmy Choo Shoes, just to name a few! We also had a slew of local vendors who participated, from hair salons to boutiques to other female-dominated services. Again, all I did was ask these companies if they would be interested in participating. They were motivated because of the direct link to *Sex and the City: The Movie and* the demographic of the audience. If you sell products or services to sophisticated and professional twenty-five- to forty-five-year-old women, and I could tell you that five hundred of them are going to be in one place all at one time, wouldn't you grab your fishing pole and starting fishing the perfect pond? Knowing the demographic you can deliver is key to strategic partnership. I didn't waste time cultivating companies that were not interested in this target market. Why spin my wheels trying to get a product for senior citizen men involved in the event when there wasn't a senior citizen man anywhere near the theatre that night? Strategic partnership is not just throwing mud at a wall and hoping it sticks. Rather it is about cultivating the right partners and putting them in front of their key target market.

When I first started planning the event, I knew I needed the media as a key partner. JPR was working hard on behalf of the event to connect with local media. This effort yielded several pre-event television interviews for me. I also felt that radio was key. So I again tapped into my courage to create an opportunity, and I reached out to one of our local radio stations, asking them to get involved. I was driving home one afternoon listening to Star 94.1 radio, and the two afternoon DJs at the time, Jenn and Rick, were talking about how excited they were about the upcoming *Sex and the City* movie. I realized that given their interest, it would make sense to reach out to them to see if they would like to get involved. I searched the radio website for their email addresses and fired off an email to Jenn. Here's the actual email I sent:

Dear Jenn,

I have been a long time listener to your afternoon radio program. I know you are getting very excited about the opening of the *Sex and the City* movie. My event management company is producing a high profile event on opening night for the movie, and I would like to invite you and Rick to be "party ambassadors." The event is going to consist of a private showing of the film and an after party at Stingaree, which will include complimentary Cosmos, VIP goodie bags, and a chance for attendees to win a pair of Jimmy Choo Shoes. All I would ask of you as a party ambassador is to talk up the event in exchange for giving away tickets on-air. I would be happy to offer the station up to twenty pairs of tickets to give away. Sounds easy, right? In addition, I would love if you and Rick would attend the event as my guests. It would be great if you both could do a welcome at the event on behalf of the radio station, and you could introduce the movie. Please let me know your thoughts—I would love to have you get involved, given your love of all things *Sex and the City!*

Within seven minutes of sending this email, Jenn responded with a resounding, "We would love to get involved!" Fabulous! I now had the radio station on the team, and with that came a publicity net that was wider than I could have ever cast on my own. How did I get one of the largest radio stations in the San Diego market involved? Simple—I asked.

What became of the radio relationship was far more than I could ever have imagined. Within a few days of getting Jenn and Rick involved, I had a call from the advertising department at Star 94.1. The account rep, Elizabeth, told me that Jenn had passed along my information, and she was super-excited to be involved with the promotion of the event. The rep went on to say that they had several of their own advertisers who had expressed interest in getting involved with the event.

Therefore, Elizabeth proposed that if they could secure enough advertisers for the station in a set period and they could offer involvement in my event as part of the advertising proposal, they would then create a thirty-second radio spot promoting my event. This was at no cost to me. Star 94.1 benefited in several ways: first, they had a great event to talk about on-air for which they could give away tickets. Radio stations love listener engagement. Second, they had an opportunity to include a value-added benefit to their advertising campaign, which would then attract new advertisers to the station. I gave away a few tickets to the station, so they could engage their listeners and in return was gifted a thirty-second radio spot as part of our partnership. This was a true give-and-take relationship on both sides. For ten days leading up to the event, a thirty-second radio spot, which was voiced by Jenn, ran on Star 94.1 up to twenty times a day. All of this started with one email to Jenn asking her and Rick to be "party ambassadors" at my event. Let me repeat: If you never ask, the answer is always no!

Between the publicity on radio and the media interest JPR was generating, it was no surprise that we sold out at almost five hundred tickets. There was literally not a seat available in the theatre on the night of the event. I owe that to the power of partnership and the courage to create my own opportunities.

The women who attended were treated to a pink carpet arrival, a goodie bag full of all kinds of treats, official *Sex and the City: The Movie* merchandise (thanks to AIM!), and a raffle ticket to win prizes and a pair of Jimmy Choo Shoes. Two local television stations ran live shots from the event on the five o'clock news and several more had footage on the eleven o'clock news that night. With the success of the event, I was walking on cloud nine in my stilettos.

Choosing to self-produce *Sex and the City: The Movie* has been a game changer for my company. I fell deeply in love with being my own client. Sure, I could have searched for a company who was willing to pay me to produce a movie premier event, but I would have just been the middleman in that case and not the conductor. I already had the tools and knowledge I needed to make it happen myself. I just needed to give myself permission to take a risk, and once I made that switch in my head, there was really no going back. The event yielded a profit of over $20,000—not too bad for just an idea!

After *Sex and the City: The Movie*, my self-producing portfolio really took off. Soon after, I produced a similar event for the movie *He's Just Not That into You*. It was a rinse and repeat of the same formula. We sold over 250 tickets to that event. As news broke of *Sex and the City 2* coming out, I started to get calls and emails asking if I was going to produce a similar event. The answer was yes, but I planned to do it in a much bigger way.

Around the time of the opening of *Sex and the City 2,* I got busy writing a handbook on how to self-produce an event based on my success from the first film. I knew that my formula could be replicated in other markets, so I set out to market my program. On the opening weekend of *Sex and the City 2*, my formula was executed by several other event planners in other markets. We had events taking place in Miami, Cincinnati, Detroit, Dallas and Fort Worth, and Los Angeles.

Remember my friend Marley, the Party Goddess? After meeting at the conference in New Orleans and her interest in my self-producing efforts, I asked Marley if she would be interested in joint-producing the event in the Los Angeles market. She agreed, and our partnership was formed. Generally, you would think that two event planners would not be interested in working together because of some arbitrary sense of competition. This was never our issue. First, Marley lives in Los Angeles, and that is two hours from San Diego, so we weren't even working in the same market. Second, Marley's target market is very different than mine, so although we are both event planners, we have very different businesses. We could bring different strengths to the partnership. Being based in LA, with a warehouse full of stage furnishings and props, Marley could contribute the local staff, client base, and décor. With my specialty in strategic partnership, I was able to secure all of the vendors and the venue. We never competed, but instead supported each other's efforts for the greater good. This was a joint-produced, sold-out event in Los Angeles.

For years, Marley has tried to crack the local news market to promote her company. Los Angeles is a very celebrity- and hard news-driven market, so unless your event falls in one of those categories, the media really aren't that interested. Although she has done national news, for some reason, her own media backyard was playing hardball. Our event was the nutcracker she needed. She was able to appear on the local LA station to promote our event. Her publicist was also able to secure a radio interview on National Public Radio (NPR).

Imagine our delight when millions of listeners heard Marley talk about the event we were joint-producing. I had friends calling me to say, "I heard The Henley Company on NPR today." In case you don't realize how big of a deal that is, the NPR website says, "Each week 26 million people listen to NPR programs and newscasts on 975 public radio stations nationwide." You can imagine the happy dance Marley and I did after her interview. She'll be the first to tell you that without our joint partnership, these media opportunities would never have come.

When thinking about events that can be self-produced, I look no further than pop culture. I pay attention to what is happening in the news and on celebrity websites. As shallow as it may seem that I start my day doing a celebrity round-up, it really is market research. I have to stay on top of trends, TV shows, musical acts, and the like that are causing a big stir. If there is big enough interest from the public in a certain book, TV show, or movie, then I start thinking about an event we can produce.

Among our other self-producing home runs have been an inaugural event for President Barack Obama and a farewell to the Oprah Show. Perhaps it was my sociology degree from UC Davis that has taught me about human nature, but I understand that as a people we like to be in a tribe or community. People could have stayed home to watch the inauguration or Oprah's last show, but the reality is that we prefer community. In both events, I created a forum for several hundred people to get together to celebrate. We sold out both events with almost three hundred guests.

One of my great joys now is teaching other event planners and executives how to self-produce an event through strategic partnerships. I have had the good fortune of coaching these individuals, and together we have created revenue-generating events for their businesses. I see opportunities for strategic partnership everywhere I turn, and it's not uncommon for me to leave a message for a friend with an idea about creating a partnership with another brand to benefit his or her business. I can't help it; I love opportunities and partnership!

Creating my own opportunities has become an important strategy for my business. I'm so fortunate that I get to share this knowledge with other business owners. Doing so provides a way to help them to view business development in a very different way. Now, entrepreneurs who are ready to stop competing and start creating their own opportunities regularly purchase my handbook and coaching program. Are you ready to give yourself permission to do the same?

As I share my story about self-producing my own events, I often get feedback from some who think it's much easier since I own an event business. Although that might be true on a cursory level, being an event planner is not the key to the success of this program. What is crucial is that I'm bold enough to ask partners to get involved. This formula really does transcend any one industry. I have no doubt that if you and I spent a few minutes together, we could make a list of dozens of ways you could partner with other businesses to benefit your business development efforts.

I'll give you a recent example. I was at Beverages & more! picking up some wine for a client event. Outside the store was a sign that talked about their upcoming beer-tasting events. I have a good friend who has recently started a company to unite the craft beer community in San Diego, which has one of the largest microbrew industries in the country, if not the world. I'm a big fan of the efforts that Brews Up is making to unite the community of craft beer drinkers.

Just by noticing what BevMo! is doing, I started thinking about my friend Nick and his company, Brews Up. In the car on the way home, I called Nick to tell him about what I saw at the store. He called me back shortly thereafter and was excited about the opportunity to connect with BevMo! Imagine what it would do for the credibility of his company if a business like BevMo! endorsed him, and they could start producing events together. It will now be up to Nick to cultivate the relationship with BevMo! I believe if he approaches them with an understanding of what they are trying to accomplish with their in-store craft beer tasting events, and Nick can illustrate how Brews Up can support their efforts, there is potential for a great relationship. The first step is for Nick to be brave enough to ask. Too many people will not give themselves permission, and they will play small. They might think there is no way a huge company like BevMo! would be interested in little ol' Brews Up. That's shallow thinking. If Nick can position himself as someone who not only helps to deliver the audience (his Brews Up community and members) but also is a partner in producing the event, that takes a huge responsibility and obligation off the BevMo! staff. This will become a win-win for both companies.

Opportunities exist everywhere; you just have to be on the lookout for them. Often they are literally right in front of your face. I was reading the *San Diego Business Journal* one day and was fascinated by an article highlighting a new Lexus car dealership that was opening in the local market. What makes this dealership different is that it is a woman-owned business, and the female owner wanted to create a hospitality center that had a car dealership as part of its service offerings. It's a change in thinking. Normally, car dealerships offer limited services, but in this case the owner wanted to flip the model. She knew that if she created a hospitality center with a top-quality restaurant, service offerings, retail stores, and a car dealership, she was going to attract the ideal client for the Lexus vehicles.

When I read the article, what caught my interest was the fact that concierge services were not listed as one of the offerings. I immediately started doing some research and sent off an email to the general manager asking if the dealership had ever considered offering concierge services as part of their service offerings. He was very kind and took an interest in my pitch. He and I met within a few weeks, and that conversation led to them asking me for a proposal outlining a comprehensive concierge program for their clients, as well as for a management contract for their on-site events. I would never have had this opportunity had I not reached out to the general manager after reading the article.

As business owners, we are taught to respond to the needs of our clients or potential clients, but I believe sometimes the potential clients need to understand why they need you. It's your job to educate them. Prior to my inquiry, the dealership had never considered having a concierge program as a value-add for their clients. I pitched, and they were interested. Nothing has been signed on the dotted line yet, but I'm certainly much further down the path than before. I am proud to have cultivated a strong relationship with the dealership, which I would not have had without creating my own opportunity to get in the door. We will see what eventually becomes of the relationship. Regardless, I know now that they know my company and are impressed with our service offerings and professionalism.

I could talk all day long about strategic partnerships as they relate to business, but you might not be someone who wants to play in the corporate sandbox the way I do. Perhaps you work in retail or you are a teacher. If that's the case, how do strategic partnerships benefit you? There is always a way!

Let's say you make delicious banana bread and you have always aspired to sell your baked goods. Why not look to partner with someone who already has a table at the local farmer's market? Wouldn't your banana bread be a great addition to the produce table? Maybe you provide samples to attendees as a way to draw them into the booth.

You could then discuss a profit-sharing opportunity with the produce company. It's a win-win for both of you. Your banana bread starts to gain attention and the produce company gets more action in its booth.

Let's say you are an expert in finances, and you have been able to relieve yourself of a significant amount of debt within a relatively short amount of time. People love to learn from success stories, so why not position yourself as the expert in debt reduction? You could partner with women's or fraternal organizations and offer to be their go-to expert. You would partner with the organization and perhaps offer a discount to their members. In return, the organization promotes your services and refers business your way. This hasn't cost you anything in terms of marketing dollars. It's really a mindset of feeling like you have something to offer that has value. Everyone knows something that is worth teaching to others. The opportunities are truly endless. There are thousands of examples I could give you about creating your own opportunities, but first you have to give yourself permission to ask, to stop competing, and to start creating. Are you ready?

I'm a big believer in microlending programs. In San Diego we have several organizations that are helping women and entrepreneurs both locally and globally to succeed. With very little access to money, women are creating businesses that are changing their families. It can be as simple as having enough money to buy a few more chickens so the woman can open an egg stand in the village. While this may never seem to us in the Western world as a way to get rich, we have to redefine our definition of success. For these women who receive microloans, having enough money to buy uniforms so their children can go to school, or enough resources to purchase a cement home instead of living in a shack defines their success. These women, in parts of the world where their opportunity to thrive is very limited, still see their value, and they figure out a way to get up every day and design a life different than the one they are living. They want more for their children, their communities, and themselves. These women have taken a risk. They have leaned on others through microlending communities to ask for help. What we might spend on a dinner with friends, these women are using to change their lives. They have given themselves permission to ask for help, and they refuse to settle or become content with their current position in society. They might not have much financially, but they do have drive, and that will get them further than anything. If these women in faraway lands with access to very few resources can see the need for creating their own opportunities and leaning on others for help, why can't you?

My intention for writing this book has never been to champion the need for all women to seek the corner office, build empires, and gain important titles. That works for some; but most women just seek happiness as their measure of success. Instead, *Permission* has been a place for me to share stories with you about my journey to success. I have also shared stories of other real women who have overcome real obstacles and challenges along the way. Although a little bruised and battered at times, they have all come out on the other side stronger than before.

You are not alone. I concur: Life can be really hard at times. There are plenty of days that I have not had the energy to face more bumps in the road. My heart has been broken beyond what I thought could ever be repaired. In fact, at times I questioned if my life would ever feel "normal" again. Whatever challenge you are facing at this moment, or insecurity you feel bathed in, I hope today you will give yourself permission to take even small steps toward designing the life you deserve. I promise once you awaken the architect in your life, there is no going back. Not every day will be easy; not every opportunity will come to fruition. But if you make just one small step in the right direction, you will finally start to live life instead of letting life live you. And that, my friends, is the true definition of happiness.

> Promise me that you'll always remember: you are braver than you believe, stronger than you seem, and smarter than you think.
>
> —Winnie the Pooh

Ask Yourself

Drive is a defining characteristic for success. What motivates you or makes you feel driven?

Is there an event you could self-produce that showcases your talent, knowledge, or expertise?

What strategic partners could you lean on? Who do you already know?

What opportunities could you create for yourself? Don't think small. Dream big and without limitations.

CHAPTER ELEVEN
Permission Granted

IF YOU NEED TO BE REMINDED THAT *YOU* HAVE THE *permission* to design the life you want to live, rip out the following *Permission Prescription* page and post it on your bathroom mirror. This will remind you every day that you can stop competing with yourself and others and start creating the opportunities you deserve!

Permission Prescription

I give myself permission to:

- » Be the architect of my own life.

- » Acknowledge and process what is keeping me locked up.

- » Commit to finding my twenty seconds of courage every day.

- » Decide which relationships need to be done and allow myself to let go.

- » Identify who is in my circle. Cherish my penthouse people and clean out my basement dwellers.

- » Create a concierge circle of like-minded, authentically supportive friends who promise to build each other up, not tear each other down.

- » Give myself daily permission to put my happiness first.

- » Identify, honor, and pursue my authentic intention.

- » Never look at "impossible" without seeing the words "I'm possible."

- » Be in love with my business and the person in the mirror. Also be in love with working hard but playing harder. I will love the people I surround myself with, and most importantly, love me more than anyone else.

- » Commit to the "big ask" and lean on others to help me design the life I want to live.

- » Create my own opportunities in life, love and business.

Permission granted!

PERMISSION GRANTED!

I give myself permission to be the architect of my own life.

I will take the following action in the next thirty days:

1.

2.

3.

4.

5.

6.

7.

8.

9.

10.

PERMISSION GRANTED!

I give myself permission to acknowledge and process what is keeping me locked up so I can move forward in my life.

I will take the following action in the next thirty days:

1.

2.

3.

4.

5.

6.

7.

8.

9.

10.

PERMISSION GRANTED!

I give myself permission to allow myself to let go of relationships that are no longer serving me well.

I will take the following action in the next thirty days:

1.

2.

3.

4.

5.

6.

7.

8.

9.

10.

PERMISSION GRANTED!

I give myself permission to identify who is in my circle. I will cherish my penthouse people and clean out my basement dwellers.

I will take the following action in the next thirty days:

1.

2.

3.

4.

5.

6.

7.

8.

9.

10.

PERMISSION GRANTED!

I give myself permission to create a concierge circle of like-minded, authentically supportive friends who promise to build each other up, not tear each other down.

I will take the following action in the next thirty days:

1.

2.

3.

4.

5.

6.

7.

8.

9.

10.

PERMISSION GRANTED!

I give myself permission to put my happiness first.

I will take the following action in the next thirty days:

1.

2.

3.

4.

5.

6.

7.

8.

9.

10.

PERMISSION GRANTED!

I give myself permission to identify, honor, and pursue my authentic intention.

I will take the following action in the next thirty days:

1.

2.

3.

4.

5.

6.

7.

8.

9.

10.

PERMISSION GRANTED!

I give myself permission to never look at "impossible" without seeing the words "I'm possible."

I will take the following action in the next thirty days:

1.

2.

3.

4.

5.

6.

7.

8.

9.

10.

PERMISSION GRANTED!

I give myself permission to

- » *Be in love with my business.*
- » *Be in love with the person in the mirror.*
- » *Work hard but play harder.*
- » *Be in love with the people I surround myself with.*
- » *Be in love with me more than anyone else.*

I will take the following action in the next thirty days:

1.

2.

3.

4.

5.

6.

7.

8.

9.

10.

PERMISSION GRANTED!

I give myself permission to commit to "The Big Ask" and lean on others to help me to design the life I want to live.

I will take the following action in the next thirty days:

1.

2.

3.

4.

5.

6.

7.

8.

9.

10.

PERMISSION GRANTED!

I give myself permission to create my own opportunities in life, love, and business.

I will take the following action in the next thirty days:

1.

2.

3.

4.

5.

6.

7.

8.

9.

10.

Epilogue

"People universally tend to think that happiness is a stroke of luck, something that will maybe descend upon you like fine weather if you are fortunate enough. But that's not how happiness works. Happiness is the consequence of personal effort. You fight for it, strive for it, insist upon it, and sometimes even travel around the world looking for it.
—Elizabeth Gilbert, author of *Eat, Pray, Love*

WHEN I WAS EIGHT YEARS OLD, MY GREAT-grandmother Rose told me that I would write a book one day. She said I had a message that the world would need to hear. A spitfire at 4 feet 10 inches and as round as she was tall, Nana was a bona fide psychic. People from all over the world looking for insight and inspiration regularly visited her.

She was feisty and naughty at times. Rarely would she wait her turn to open presents on Christmas Day. On more than one occasion, she stole cherry tomatoes off the salads at restaurants and hid them in her purse. Nana was not a carnival psychic or a tarot card reader. Believe me, there were no circus acts going on in her reading room. Rather, her space was a solace for people to connect with those they had lost and to find direction. She had a kindness about her that could change the energy in every room she entered. Nana had a great gift to connect with those on the other side and was chosen to share their messages.

I realize that not everyone understands or believes in psychics or intuitives. Had I not grown up with this practice as a very real and authentic piece of my childhood, I might be a skeptic, too. Given my experience, when Nana told me that I would one day write a book, I chose to believe her. I have used writing and story-sharing as therapy for many years. I realize that every experience has led me to the place I am now sitting, in front of my MacBook Pro, putting the finishing touches on a book that essentially wrote itself.

I met a literary agent, Ariela Wilcox of the Wilcox Agency, and with trepidation asked her to take a look at some of my writing. She validated my writing ability, and in less than two months from that initial meeting, I wrote the entire book. This journey has changed my life. She gave me the permission I needed to write the book. See—even I need reassurance and validation now and again!

This book evolved out of the feedback I was getting from women in the audience at my presentations. I thought making one woman cry during my presentation was a fluke. Everyone has an emotional day. But then the line started getting longer, with more women crying and being moved by the content. As I was giving presentations around the country, more women kept mentioning the word *permission*. Something I was saying was touching their permission nerve. I was perplexed as to why they didn't feel like they had permission to design the life they wanted before they heard my speech.

As I talked to more women and got to know them personally, I learned that they felt stuck in their lives. Whatever had happened up to that day was keeping them locked up. I'm sure they enjoyed hearing about my working at the Olympics, living in London, running a business, and enjoying fabulous experiences. Still, what really resonated with these women were the struggles I had faced. I have not had perfect relationships; I've not always liked myself. My self-esteem fluctuates.

I've cried. I've been depressed. I've been sideways financially. I've boomeranged home to live with my parents at an age where most of my friends are married and have young families. I've taken the long way around.

That's my story, but it's not all doom and gloom. Nothing brings you clarity about how far you have come in life than to commit to vulnerability and writing your story. It would be easy to blame my crazy life on the men I've loved and lost, the struggles in business, or the friends that have disappointed me profoundly. However, those are just accessories to the life I have chosen to live. I'm not a victim; I'm just a girl trying to make sense of love, life, and the pursuit of happiness. But along the way, I figured out that creating my own opportunities, cleaning out the basement-dweller friends, identifying my authentic intention, and then asking others for help were the best strategies for success. If this book can help you to discover the same, then the hours I have spent in front of my laptop have been well worth it.

What surprised me the most about writing *Permission* was how deep into my soul this journey took me and how quickly memories that were long buried from childhood began to surface. Writing a book has been one of the most personally revealing activities I have ever experienced. Throughout this journey, I had to give myself permission to deal with the skeletons. Only recently did I find the courage to share with my family some deep-rooted secrets that I realized have probably been subconscious roadblocks for far too long. Giving myself permission to finally speak my truth has been emotionally rewarding as part of this journey. I thought for far too long that I should have to bear my burdens alone. But as I began writing and championing the need to lean on others for help, I realized I had to take my own advice. I could no longer authentically write *Permission* if indeed I was just going to pretend everything was fine.

There's that word *fine* again; oh, how I dislike thee! Everything was *not* fine, nor was it just okay, nor was it content. My architect decided it was time to open my mouth and let my heart speak.

As I finally unveiled my emotional scar to my family, I could feel the healing begin. Their validation was significant to shedding the layers of shame. You may feel like I did: that your demons are best kept buried, but the reality is that the truth will always find you. I encourage you to tell someone, so you can move to a place of healing. Otherwise, you give the hurt way too much power.

Think of what you could accomplish with the energy you have given to your pain by trying to suppress it. Give yourself permission to tell just one person: your therapist, a confidant, or a family member. In business matters, I always champion telling many people what you are trying to accomplish so they can help you. But private matters are different. They are deep and raw, and you do not need to tell the world; just one penthouse person will do.

My professional life is going very well. This year The Henley Company will turn seven years old, and it will forever be the greatest labor of love I have ever committed to. Coaching fellow entrepreneurs and students on how to design the life they want to live has been a great addition to my professional course. I keep my head down and my drive moving forward as I build my empire. I'm not one who has to announce on Facebook that we are signing up clients right and left and that we are exhausted by every conference call they make. Some people need the validation from their Facebook family more than I do. That's their prerogative, and I hope they find their penthouse people through likes and status updates. Instead, I'm carving my path in a determined and intentional way.

I have huge goals for The Henley Company, which include licensing and partnerships galore. But my true focus is really being in love with my life. I admit that I still struggle a bit when I tell people I live with my parents, because at my age that is just not something that you should do—or so they say. I've told my family that once I put a mini fridge in my childhood bedroom and start collecting cats, it's time for a true intervention. Until then, I'm going to soak up every perfect moment of laughter, love, and memory-making that we require in this family.

By living at home, I've been far more involved in the lives of my niece and nephew, Elyse and Ian. Instead of seeing them maybe once a week, I now see them on a regular basis because they live so close to our house. Watching them grow into fine young humans gives me great perspective on how quickly time passes. In addition, I also get to see more of my sister, Jodi, and her husband Steve, both of whom I adore. I cherish these moments with them and know that if my address were elsewhere I would never have had this time with them.

Yes, I do plan on eventually moving out and back into my own place. Right now, with the amount of travel I'm doing and the extended weeks I am away from home, this works. Where I live during this chapter will matter little on the day of reckoning. What I will remember will be the weeknight dinners, glasses of wine, story-telling, and memory-making that my family values beyond where I list my address. You can mock me for choosing to live at home, but I will never trade this time for all the independence and money in the world. I love my penthouse family, and I've given myself permission to be okay with living at home.

Beyond releasing *Permission* to the world, I am hoping that it is the launch of something special in our communities. It's time we start leaning on each other and becoming a true village. I believe strongly in the power of the concierge circles. In historic times, a concierge was defined as the "keeper of the candle and the keys." Concierges were the people that met visiting noblemen at the door and let them into the castle. They were the ones that attended to all of the needs of the guests. In simple terms, they are the helpers.

In my own business, we define a concierge as a lifestyle manager for busy executives and their families. We oversee their to-do lists and execute projects and details on their behalf. For us, being a concierge is a motivation for helping people to embrace more time for recess. If we can manage their to-do list, it gives them more time to enjoy life. I realize that not everyone can afford the services of a concierge, but there is no reason why we can't create circles in our communities where we can be helpers for others. I would like to see concierge circles flourish like book clubs have. Then, instead of women gathering under the pretense of actually reading a book (translation—an opportunity to get together to drink wine!), we are getting together to see how we can authentically support each other. Wine still required, of course!

In the past, I have been disheartened with women (more than one, unfortunately) who start organizations to support other women and then become unethical. However, I still believe that the army of women is the strongest force of all. If you are looking for help, consult your concierge circle. If you are in need of errands being run, lean on your circle and share the responsibility. Look to your circle to plan special experiences for families and the neighborhood. Together we can create a movement of women helping each other to create opportunities instead of competing against each other. I'm not saying we all need to live in a Namaste, down-dog world, where we all eat granola in our communes and take time for meditation. Competition is vital; it's how we are wired as humans. Nor do I agree that we shouldn't keep score at soccer games for children because it might hurt little feelings when they lose. I'm the adult in the stands who knows exactly how many goals were scored by each team. And I don't believe everyone should have the number 1 on their uniforms because we are all winners. We aren't. Not every time, at least, but that doesn't mean we shouldn't give it a valiant fight every day.

My need to be a cheerleader for creating rather than competing comes from a self-serving position. If you stop competing with yourself—your childhood, your demons, your self-esteem, your weight, your baggage carried over from bad relationship—it's amazing how you turn on your creativity. You certainly don't need to pick up a paint brush and create a masterpiece, but when you look at your life through creative eyes in terms of opportunity, authentic intention, and seeing the words, "I'm possible" instead of *impossible*, the entire world looks different. I'm tired of the internal competition, and instead have chosen to draw a line in the sand. I'm no longer going to give in to fear but instead will live fearlessly. The trench coat of burden you might be wearing will become last year's fashion, and instead you will take on the runway of life in a very productive and authentic new outfit.

This is my hope for you as the reader of _Permission_. I can't wait for you to share with me the difference that giving yourself permission has made in your life. In fact, I look forward to writing my second book, which will highlight the journeys of women who moved from locked to unlocked and are thriving, having started by giving themselves permission.

As we part ways, remember permission is the only thing keeping you stagnant and from designing the life you want to live. Go be bold. Be brave. Let your authentic intention be a gift to the world. I give you permission to be fearless and fabulous.

Resources

WHAT INSPIRES ME? CHECK OUT THESE WEBSITES, people, resources, and books that I turn to for inspiration, creativity, and designing my best life.

Get Inspired

Simon T. Bailey, *The Brilliance Institute*, http://www.SimonTBailey.com
Richard Branson, http://www.virgin.com/richard-branson
Gary Vaynerchuk, http://www.garyvaynerchuk.com/
Steve Jobs's Commencement Address, Stanford University, 2005
Ted Talks, http://www.Ted.com
Marley Majcher, The Party Goddess, http://www.ThePartyGoddess.com

Get Reading

Marley Majcher, *But Are You Making Any Money?*
Bethanny Frankle, *The Place of Yes*
Michael Gerber, *The E-Myth Revisited*
Dr. Heidi Hannah, *The Sharp Solution*
Drs. Kevin and Jackie Freiberg, *Guts.*
Entrepreneur Magazine
Fast Company Magazine

Get Help

Professional Organizations—Event Industry
International Special Events Society
International Concierge and Lifestyle Management Association
Meeting Planners International
Public Relations Society of America

Professional

Communications Works, Inc., http://www.CommunicationWorksInc.com
J Public Relations, http://www.JPublicRelations.com
University of San Diego, Event Management Certificate Program, http://www.SanDiego.edu/emp

Get Creative

Event Design and Inspiration
Ceci New York, http://www.CeciNewYork.com
Hostess with the Mostess, http://www.HostessWithTheMostess.com
Pinterest, http://www.Pinterest.com/Henleyco

Photography

Helene Cornell Photography, http://www.helenecornell.com

Author Biography

NICOLE R. MATTHEWS, CSEP, IS FOUNDER AND lifestyle architect of The Henley Company, a woman-owned business based in San Diego, but operating wherever her passport takes her. Nicole founded The Henley Company in 2007 after a long career as a corporate event planner. With the belief that life should be experienced in a big way, Nicole set out to create a company focused on helping clients to live the life they want and to produce the experiences they want to remember. She believes that recess is not just for elementary school kids.

For that reason, The Henley Company was established as a portal for clients to enjoy more events and travel, and to add to their lifestyle experiences. With over fourteen years of event management and marketing experience, she has produced a long list of distinguished events for notable organizations, both nationally and internationally.

Nicole not only works with clients to create unique experiences, significant celebrations, and memory-making events, but also is recognized as a leader in self-producing events and strategic partnerships. Nicole has self-produced numerous high-profile events, original concepts promoted to targeted demographics. Her *Sex and the City: The Movie* premier became a landmark event that established her reputation as an expert in self-producing events. The event was so successful that she franchised the concept to event planners in other markets so they could self-produce events around the opening of *Sex and the City 2*.

Nicole now coaches planners about the benefits of self-producing and owning their events, and the value of strategic partnership. In addition, she mentors other concierge businesses on building their brands and establishing their market differential.

Active in her industry, Nicole is a past president of the San Diego chapter of the International Special Events Society (ISES) and is one of only 350 professionals in the world to hold the Certified Special Events Professional (CSEP) designation. She has earned a certificate in event management from the University of San Diego and George Washington University Event Management Program, a BA in sociology from the University of California, Davis, and a MA in educational leadership from the University of San Diego. Nicole is an adjunct professor at Mesa College in San Diego, and an instructor in the University of San Diego's Certificate in Event Management program, where she teaches the next generation of event professionals.

Nicole's noteworthy professional achievements include: nominee, ISES Esprit Award, granted to the best and brightest in the special events industry; nominee, Women Who Mean Business award; recipient of the TWIN award, granted by the YWCA of San Diego; recipient of 40 Under 40 award, granted by *San Diego Metropolitan Magazine*; nominee, Women Who Move the City, presented by *San Diego Magazine*; and recipient of Instructor of the Year by the University of San Diego Event Management Certificate program.

Nicole's ultimate experience was working at the London 2012 Olympics, and she managed a corporate VIP program at the 2013 Super Bowl. She spent the summer of 2013 working the FIFA Confederation Cup in Brazil, and in January 2014, she worked in Sochi, Russia, at the Winter Olympic Games.

Nicole lives in San Diego with her fabulous family and favorite beach companion, her golden retriever Simon. She has refused to give up on love now that she has fallen completely in love with herself. She is already busy working on her next book, *How Big is Your Bold?*, a collection of stories about women who gave themselves permission to thrive.

Acknowledgements

AS THE CHAMPION OF ASKING FOR HELP AND LEANING
on others for support, it will come as no surprise that I have numerous
people to thank as I put the final touches on *Permission*, my very first
book.

Thank-you to Ariela Wilcox of The Wilcox Agency, my literary
agent, cheerleader and permission giver. Ariela and I randomly met
at an executive meeting. Within ten days I had taken the first step on
this epic sprint of book writing. She gave me six weeks; I thought she
was crazy. She was right because that was all I needed. I wrote; she
edited. I doubted; she picked my chin up. I gained confidence; she
kept molding me to be better. There is little doubt that I could have
done this without her help. I would still be talking instead of doing.
We would meet weekly for our sessions at a tiny table in Barnes &
Noble, and I prayed for inspiration from the books staring back at
me. I gulped when she would turn each page, and we would talk
about her edits and notes. There was a day when she flipped through
seven pages without one edit. For a girl who got "Oh, vomit" stamped
on her advanced English literature paper by her teacher, this was a
major accomplishment. Ariela has learned to love (or pretends to) the
importance of validating me with happy face on my papers! Thank

you, Ariela. You have been the best therapist, cheerleader, and agent this first-time author could ever ask for.

Thank-you to my students and event colleagues. You continue to inspire me to be better at my craft, to work harder, and to be a trailblazer in our industry.

Thank-you to my small but mighty group of women I am lucky enough to call friends. Lisa—you are my sunshine, and I can never thank you enough for giving me a second chance after my deplorable first impression. You have supported me without judgment, turned my tears into smiles on way too many occasions, and allowed me to share in the joy of your beautiful family. I could not love you more if I tried.

Marley—you are a mentor who has become a dear friend. We have the great ability to always pick up where we left off and to find the humor in every wacky situation one of us has found herself in. I doubt you will ever really know the depth of your contribution to the special events industry and female entrepreneurs. We all run our businesses smarter and focus on making substantial money thanks to you. I have learned more from you than I am sure I have ever taught. I have also enjoyed every minute of being in your company since the first time we had coffee in a Starbucks in San Diego when we talked about joint-producing our first event together. Since then we have traveled together, experienced several boondoggles, and analyzed more episodes of *Real Housewives* than two grown women should. I wouldn't want it any other way. *Thank-you* for choosing me to be in your life.

Marcy—where do I even begin? Little did I know that my sister's college friend would eventually become one of my best friends! If we could propel ourselves with the energy from the laughter we have shared, we would have gone to the moon and back already. I adore every ounce of your being. You are my truth, and I know we have shared things with each other that only we know. I can't imagine my life without you. The miles between us are no divide for the depth of our friendship. *Thank-you* for being you.

Thank-you to Ian and Beverley. By inviting me to share your office space, you helped my business to thrive. Your friendship and generosity continue to humble me. What a gift it is to share in the joy of your beautiful family, and to watch your children evolve into gracious young people. I have told you many times how much I appreciate the tremendous opportunity you gave me by opening up your office to me. Still, I doubt the words will ever convey the depths of my gratitude. Sharing the soccer sidelines years ago may have brought us together as friends, but respect, gratitude, and the deepest appreciation for your kind hearts, love of laughter, and a good sing-along have made you both family.

Thank-you to Beverly P. Your friendship has become an unbelievable gift out of a situation that I thought I would never survive. Your support of me, my heart and my journey has become so important to my soul. You are the only one that really understands "him" and what that relationship meant to me. He will forever be your brother, but for a chapter, he was everything to me. You never judged; you never questioned; you always were my cheerleader, and could see my love was authentic. Out of all the hurt, I earned your friendship, and for that I will be forever grateful. Now it's your turn to give yourself permission to live the life you want. I aim to be the loudest penthouse cheerleader you've ever had!

Thank-you to Becca. My dearest Becca. We started as neighbors back in 1975, and today we are closer than sisters. I am lucky that I have never known life without you being an important part of it. Together we have lived through the highest highs and the lowest lows. Our lives could not be more different: You are the mother of four amazing children, married to a great man and are a smarty-pants who has the answer to every scientific question I have. Where as, I'm trying to find a man I like long enough to keep around! I'm also trying to keep my ovaries functioning long enough before they expire due to age. Lastly, I can only outsmart you when it comes to celebrity gossip. Regardless of what we have faced, we always have had each other. You are a fantastic mother, wife, and a professor to thousands of students lucky to have you as their teacher. To be the godmother of little Brooklyn is an honor I will always treasure. *Thank-you* for being my everything.

Thank-you to Ray and Marjorie. Every time I do a stint in England, you make sure the door is always open, the kettle is on, and the back bedroom is ready for me. Little did I know when my sister Jodi married into your family that I would end up with two remarkable people in my life. I can't thank you enough for your love and support and for always being my home away from home in the mighty UK. Ray—you left us too soon, my friend. I promise we will all look after Marjorie in your stead.

Thank-you to Steve-o, the brother-in-law of all B-I-Ls. We joke that you are married to sister wives because of how much time I spend with you and Jodi. When we met, I was just eighteen years old, and you still had a full head of hair. Since then, I've grown up and you're practically bald. You are more than just my B-I-L; you are one of my best friends. When my heart has broken, you were the shoulder I needed to cry on. When I come up with a crazy idea, you are my reality and rain on my parade. When I need a playmate, you are my plus one. I can't imagine Jodi being married to someone who completes her more than you do. Thank you for taking amazing care of my sister, blessing me with a beautiful niece and nephew, and for being the brother I have never had. You are the piece that completes our family puzzle.

Thank-you to Jodi. Now the tears have started! Shocker, I know! A few years ago, you gave me a plaque that says, "How do people make it through life without a sister?" I have no idea, and am so grateful that I have never had to find out. We are two peas in a pod, so much so that sometimes we show up in the same exact outfit. You can make me laugh harder than anyone, and are the person I want to spend the most time with. I will always be the person you can call on when you get your finger stuck trying on rings at the store, or the person you have to lean on when the blackness comes and you slip down the wall when you smell the hospital. You have certainly tough-loved me through relationships and helped me to pick up the pieces on more than one occasion. You eased into motherhood with expertise and have provided a wonderful life for Ian and Elyse. They are lucky to call you Mom. You are indeed my best friend, and I love you beyond words.

Thank-you to Ian and Elyse—my pride and joy. How lucky I am to be able to be your aunt and to share in your special lives. I am deeply proud of the young adults you are growing into, and the way you treasure our special family time. I hope you always are brave and bold and you never think small. The world is a big place; promise me you will go out and experience as much of it as you can. Love your friends. Cherish your sibling. Be kind to all people and don't ever sweat the small stuff. You both can accomplish anything you want. Why? Because you know you will always have the safety net of this crazy, supportive family. If there is ever a day that I could be blessed with children of my own, I would be the luckiest mom on the planet if they are as fabulous as you two are to me. I love you both to the moon and back and around the world one more time!

Thank-you to my mom and dad. There are never words profound enough to thank you for all of your love and support. You have ensured that our home was indeed home base. Regardless of where my travels take me, I always know that your dinner table on a Sunday night is the best restaurant in the world, and there is no place I would rather be. You are my greatest cheerleaders, my best support system, and two of the most dynamic and kind people I will ever meet. Lucky for me, in addition to all that, I get to call you Mom and Dad. You have raised Jodi and me to be strong, independent women, but to never lose sight of the value of family. I know what we have is special. The only way I can even come close to repaying you for the tremendous life you have provided us is to continue to make you proud. You have given me permission to live my best life, and it's the best gift I could ever ask for. I could never get by without you, so please promise you will live forever! I love you—I love you—I love you!

And finally, *thank-you* to all of the women who have inspired me to write this book, and who have been inspired by my stories. Please give yourself permission to always design the life you want to live. Stop competing with yourself and start creating your own opportunities. Being in control is a wonderful feeling! We have unleashed the century of women, and together we can indeed change the world. Please join me in the journey.

> She believed she could, so she did.
>
> —Author Unknown